MASTER CLASS

COUNTRY Guitar

A Guide to Playing Modern & Traditional Electric Country Lead Guitar

by AL BONHOMME

To access audio, visit:
www.halleonard.com/mylibrary

Enter Code
7932-7748-8622-8463

ISBN 978-0-6340-3434-3

HAL•LEONARD®
CORPORATION

7777 W. BLUEMOUND RD. P.O. BOX 13819 MILWAUKEE, WI 53213

Visit Hal Leonard Online at
www.halleonard.com

Table of Contents

Introduction

Country guitar is a huge style encompassing many different sub-genres, techniques, sounds, and rhythms. It also combines deceivingly difficult simplicity with mind-boggling technical wizardry. And it does so with style. This book's main focus is on electric guitar—including pick style and hybrid picking—in both traditional and modern country guitar playing.

This is not just a collection of hot licks; each chapter explores a different aspect, technique, or concept of country guitar playing. Some involve specific playing techniques like string bending or hybrid picking; other chapters look at different styles or more theoretical concepts, such as which scale to use over which chord, etc. The material is presented in an order that loosely builds upon itself as you go through the book, but you do not necessarily have to follow the order to get a lot out of it. Typically, a concept is discussed and a few demonstrative licks are shown, followed by a complete solo focusing on the same topic.

Some of the techniques may take you a little time to develop. It's OK to learn one short lick from one chapter and keep working on it as your technical skill develops. In the meantime, you can start working on something else from a different chapter that uses a completely different concept. You can also approach the book as just a lot of individual licks if you'd like. Even the longer solos can be broken down into a series of individual ideas to learn separately. Please keep in mind that I do think it's a good idea to learn complete solos, as it aids in developing a sense of continuity and phrasing in your playing.

Ultimately, the act of listening is going to be your best teacher. I would encourage you to seek out and listen to the great country artists and guitar players, past and present. Steal all you can and morph their ideas into your own. Hopefully, this book will whet your appetite, open a few new doors, and inspire you to new levels of creativity in your country pickin'!

About the Author

Al Bonhomme is a Los Angeles-based guitar player, producer, songwriter, and teacher. He records and performs regularly throughout the Southern California area. His recording and performance credits include Dwight Yoakam, Pete Anderson, Deana Carter, Mark Collie, Danni Leigh, Scott Josh, Al Bruno, Dale Watson, Johnny Highland, Albert Lee, Liona Boyd, Terri Binion, Jim Matt, George Highfill, "The Tonight Show with Jay Leno," "The Grand Ole Opry," "Crook and Chase," TNN, Disney Entertainment, and many more Southern California artists.

He's written intructional articles featured in *Guitar Player*, *Guitar World*, and *Acoustic Guitar* magazines and is an instructor at Musicians Institute in Hollywood, California, specializing in country guitar and acoustic guitar styles. Al can be contacted at his website: **www.albonhomme.com**

Chapter One:
1 Pentatonic Scales

The pentatonic scale is ubiquitious in country music. Specifically, major pentatonic scales are the most common scale forms generally associated with the style and many of its sub-genres. Although there are many other scales and note choices, a basic major pentatonic scale will give you the safest, most "inside-sounding" notes to use for country-flavored soloing. It also offers you an ideal way to anchor your playing while developing more harmonically complex melodic ideas. A country guitarist needs to be very familiar with both major and minor pentatonic ideas in all keys—everywhere on the guitar neck.

The Major Pentatonic Scale

A major pentatonic scale is comprised of five notes derived from the major scale. The 1st, 2nd, 3rd, 5th, and 6th degrees of the major scale will form its corresponding major pentatonic. The best way to become familiar with pentatonic scales on the guitar is to learn movable patterns, which can then be transposed to any key without changing the fingering.

Relative Major and Minor Scales

Another very important bit of music theory is to understand the relationship between major and minor scales. Relative major and minor scales use the exact same notes and key signature. The only difference is the root, or starting note (also known as the tonic).

In a C major scale (C–D–E–F–G–A–B), for example, the first note (C) is the relative major, and the 6th note (A) is the relative minor. Therefore, this same scale could also be an A natural minor scale. The easy way to understand this concept is to remember that C major = A minor and then transpose that concept to other keys. In other words:

- F major = D minor
- G major = E minor
- B♭ major = G minor, etc.

The more you practice this, the easier it becomes. Many times, a Circle of 5ths diagram will reflect this in key signatures.

A practical approach to this with regard to the guitar is to put four fingers down on consecutive frets of one string. Your first finger is on the relative minor note, and your fourth finger is on the relative major note. If you put your first finger on an A note (the relative minor), your fourth finger will be on a C note (the relative major).

This comes in very handy because you'll find that a lick you learned in C major also works over an A minor chord (and vice versa), thus doubling the places where you can play most licks you know.

Learn all pentatonic scale patterns and work on converting them to the relative minor/major.

How to Use Pentatonic Scales

The simplest, most direct application of the scale is to use the matching pentatonic of the key in which you are playing. As long as the chord progression remains diatonic (i.e., all the chords are in the key), this will generally work well. Let's check out a progression in G major.

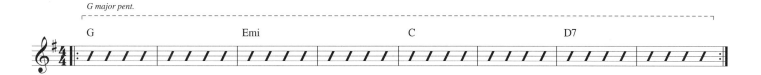

Using G major pentatonic over the C chord leaves out the C note, which is an essential chord tone (the root). Therefore, the best pentatonic choice here would be C major pentatonic. The same thing applies to the D7 chord. Using G major pentatonic, you are leaving out a F♯, which is the 3rd of a D major chord. The best pentatonic choice here would be D major pentatonic. So, here's a better rule: use the matching major pentatonic scale of any major chord.

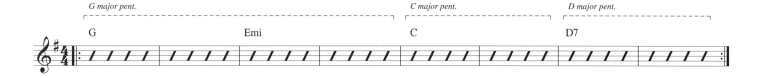

This same rule can be applied to minor chords: use the matching minor pentatonic of any minor chord.

Bear in mind that this rule can begin to wear out its welcome if it sounds as though you're making drastic position shifts for each chord. The idea is to learn your scale patterns all over the neck, in every key, and to make changes between scales without obvious shifts. Your ideas should flow into each other melodically without having to jump to a new position for every chord.

Also, sometimes it does sound good to stay in one pentatonic scale. Try this progression, staying in E minor pentatonic, as well as changing to different pentatonic scales as indicated. You can also mix and match.

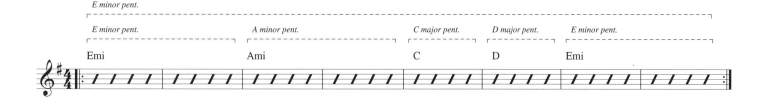

Using pentatonic scales in this way will help target chord tones, which will make your playing sound solid and harmonically informed—much like a jazz player but in a simpler manner. The same rule applies to non-diatonic chords. Use the matching pentatonic scale of the non-diatonic chord.

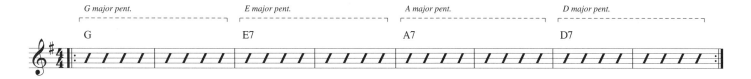

Obviously, there are other note and scale choices you could make, but this is a good way to begin playing over chord changes in country music.

Minor pentatonic scales also sound good over major chords in the right situations. Doing this gives you a bluesy tonality with a funky or rock edge. The tune you are playing dictates if this will work or not. You can hear this in a lot of classic traditional country, as well as the modern rockin' country music. (Note that G minor pentatonic over the C major chord sounds good, too).

Mix and Match

It also can be effective to switch between major and minor pentatonics over individual chords (or a chord progression) to maintain variety in your playing. A ♭3rd in major and a ♭5th in major or minor are commonly used as passing tones. Melody always supersedes any scale pattern you might be using, even if the note is completely outside of the scale pattern. Don't be afraid to follow your ear and take a chance!

Check out the intro to "Chattahoochie" by Alan Jackson or "Ramblin' Fever" by Merle Haggard for some major pentatonic ideas. "Guitars and Cadillacs" by Dwight Yoakam or "Don't Rock the Jukebox" by Alan Jackson demonstrate many combined major and minor pentatonics.

Major Pentatonic Licks

Now let's check out some licks using the major pentatonic. This first example shows a typical melody based on the extended C major pentatonic scale.

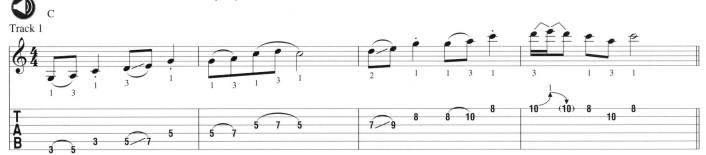

This example uses the extended A major pentatonic scale.

This lick uses D major pentatonic. Note the use of the F♮ note (the minor 3rd of D) to slur into the F♯ note (the major 3rd).

Track 3

This lick uses C major pentatonic throughout.

Track 4

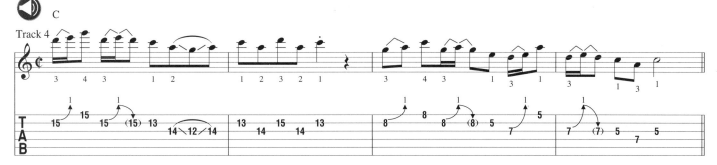

Minor Pentatonic Licks

These minor pentatonic licks can work over a minor or major chord tonality. Try hybrid picking (pick and fingers) for a chicken-pickin' sound.

This is an A minor pentatonic lick.

Track 5

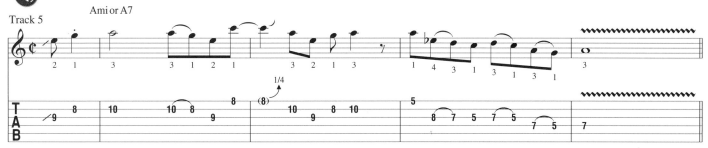

This is a G minor pentatonic idea.

Track 6

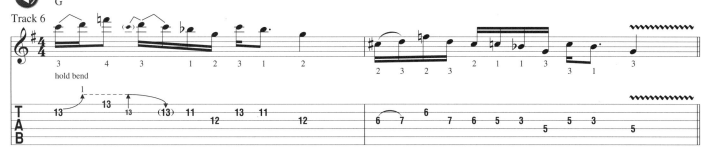

This lick makes use of E minor pentatonic. Try this lick over E7. Experiment with hybrid and flatpicking, and let the first few notes ring into each other.

Track 7

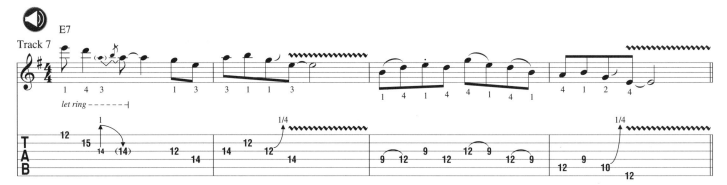

This lick is based off A minor pentatonic pattern #4. You can use it for a funky A7 sound or over an A minor chord.

Track 8

Pentatonic Solo

This solo is mainly constructed with major pentatonic scales and demonstrates how they can be used to fit the chord changes in a song. Over each chord of the tune, the corresponding major pentatonic scale is used. This facilitates hitting the good-sounding chord tones and makes your playing sound harmonically grounded. Also prominently displayed is the common practice of bending up to the 3rd (from the 2nd) and the 6th (from the 5th) degrees of the scale, as well as pre-bending (i.e., bending a note before picking it, then picking it and releasing it down). A ♭3rd note is often used to hammer onto or slide into a major 3rd, as in bar 13.

If this were a solo over a real song, you wouldn't have to stick so rigidly to just pentatonic scales. As you become more adept at using them, you can depart from pentatonics often, but by familiarizing yourself with them first, you'll always have a solid-sounding home base to which you can return at any time.

Pent Sounds

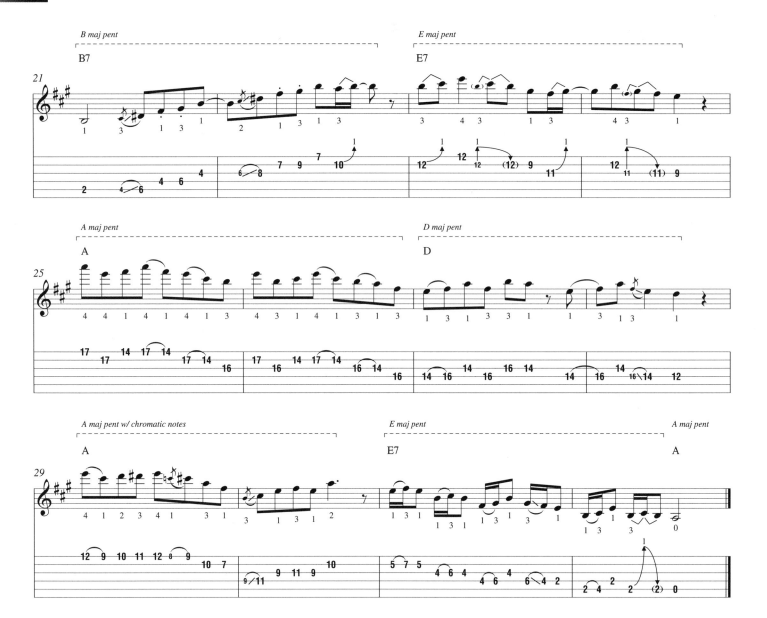

Big Dog Blues

This solo demonstrates the way in which major and minor pentatonic scales can be combined to create a more interesting solo in the style of Don Rich or Roy Nichols. The minor pentatonic scale imparts a bluesy, funky sound, while the major pentatonic scale sounds more diatonic and inside. Notice how small portions of the different pentatonic scales are used and moved around to fit the chord changes.

Try using hybrid picking for a chicken-pickin' effect. At bar 12, the C hexatonic/mixolydian scale is a major sound with a ♭7th.

Chapter Two: Other Scales
2

The vast majority of country songs tend to be in major keys. When playing country guitar, you always have to be aware of two things: the **key** and the **chord**. This is much like jazz but usually with less sophisticated harmony. Depending on those two things, many scales other than the pentatonic can be—and often are—used in country guitar.

The Major Scale

Having a good, solid major scale foundation will help you unravel your guitar neck and enable you to tie many different concepts and ideas together—in any key, anywhere on your guitar. The major scale is composed of seven notes. Starting on a tonic of C, it gives us the following notes: C–D–E–F–G–A–B. The notes then repeat themselves up or down an octave until you run out of frets or strings.

All major scales, in every key, follow the same intervallic pattern of whole steps (two frets) and half steps (one fret): whole–whole–half–whole–whole–whole–half. On the guitar, this lends itself to movable scale patterns. You can learn a scale in one position and then move the exact same pattern to another position on the neck. As you move the scale around, the tonic note of the scale changes.

For example, if you play a C major scale pattern and then move that exact pattern up two frets, it becomes a D major scale. The same pattern up three more frets would become an F major scale.

How to Use Major Scales in Country Guitar

Using major scales is relatively simple. As long as the chords remain diatonic, you can use the major scale that corresponds to the key of the song. You should, however, be aware of the chord tones for each chord. To make your melodic statements solid and effective, you should always try to follow the chords with your note choices.

Don't limit yourself to one static scale pattern either. Connecting the different patterns of the same key will allow your lines to flow effortlessly from one range to another. You'll have to combine them in different ways to accommodate the melodic flow, depending on the fingerings of what you are playing.

Notes of the C Major Scale

When we build a triad (three-note chord) off every note in the scale, we are *harmonizing the scale*. In the harmonized C major scale, the following are the seven resultant diatonic chords.

Note: the B° (or B diminished) chord is not often used as the vii chord. A ♭VII chord—B♭ in this case—is much more commonly used in country than the diatonic B° chord.

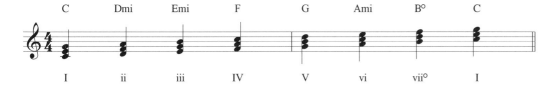

All of the chords in the following progression are diatonic to the key of C major. You could use a C major scale over the whole thing.

Non-diatonic Chords

A non-diatonic chord is one that does not appear in the harmonized major scale of the key. The three most common non-diatonic chords in country are:

- **Major or dominant II chord:** In the key of C, this would be D or D7.
- **Major ♭VII chord** (as mentioned on the previous page): In the key of C, this would be B♭.
- **Major ♭III chord:** In the key of C, this would be E♭.

In the following progression in the key of C, the D7, B♭, and E♭ are not diatonic. Over the D7 chord, use the D Mixolydian mode. The Mixolydian mode is just like the major scale, but it has a ♭7th degree. So, D Mixolydian is spelled: D–E–F♯–G–A–B–C.

Over the B♭ chord, use C Mixolydian (C–D–E–F–G–A–B♭).

And over the E♭ chord, use the C minor (or E♭ major) scale (C–D–E♭–F–G–A♭–B♭). These situations will be analyzed a little deeper in upcoming chapters. See scale patterns, Chapter 15.

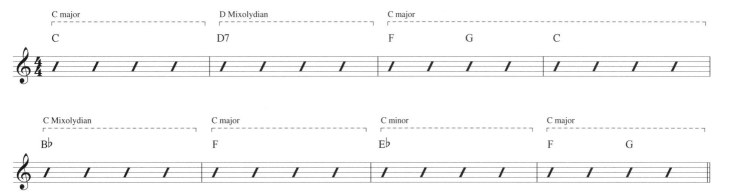

Chromatic Notes

A *chromatic* note is a note that occurs in-between two scale tones. Chromatic notes are commonly used as passing tones as you play a solo or melody. They help to make your playing sound less predictable and inside. Let your ear guide you. Try to stick to scale or chord tones on the strong beats and the points of resolution.

All of the notes below marked with a sharp (♯) are chromatic notes since they fall in-between the diatonic scale tones.

Shuffle Up and Deal

This solo, played in the style of a classic Ray Price shuffle, demonstrates the use of major scales combined with chromatic notes, which add a little more color. If you stick strictly to the confines of any one scale, your playing will sound predictable and not hold interest. A solo using a complete major scale will tend to sound more linear than a strictly pentatonic solo.

When using major scale ideas, the fingerings may seem a little strange at first if you are used to pentatonics. If you lighten up on your left hand, it may help you make the transition. Pay attention to how the notes are used to outline the chords tones. If you play this solo without any backing chords, you can still hear the chord changes.

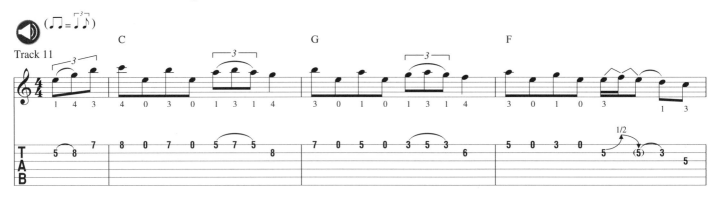

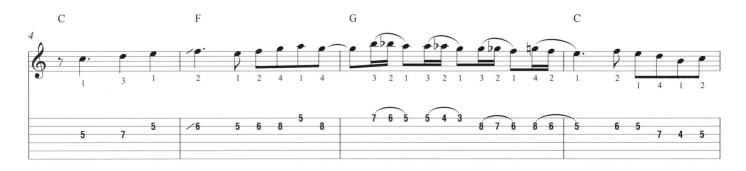

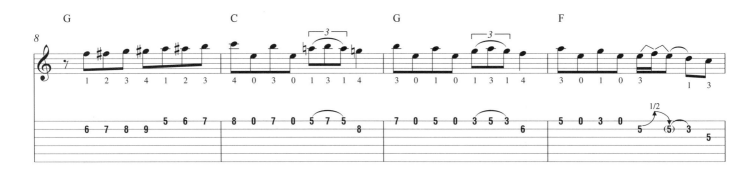

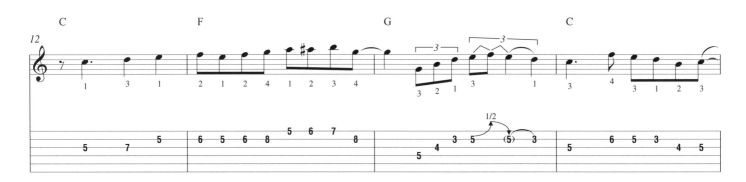

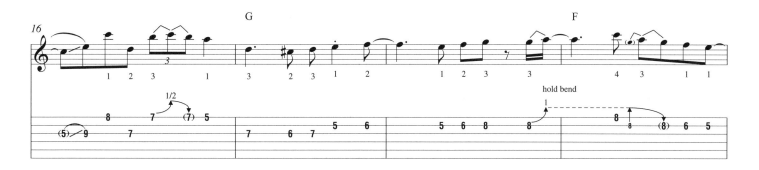

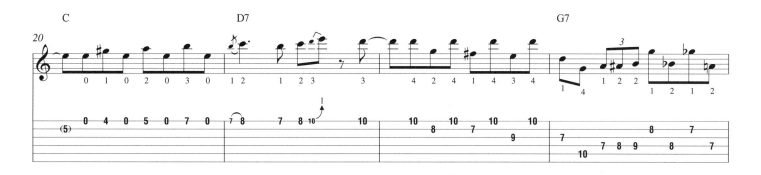

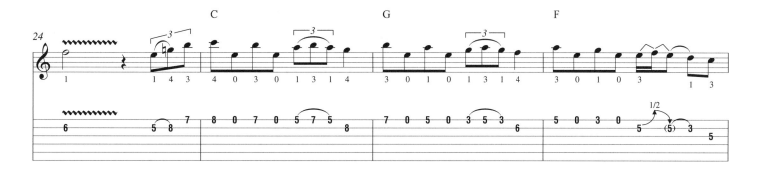

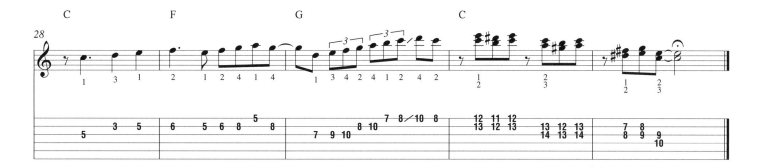

Mixolydian (Dominant 7th) Mode

The Mixolydian mode is like the major scale but with a ♭7th note. In the key of C, for example, you would change the B note to a B♭ to get the C Mixolydian mode. This scale works perfectly over unaltered dominant 7th and 9th chords. It sounds a little on the funky side, but it can make a blues tune sound a little happier because of the major 3rd as opposed to minor blues scales.

As a general rule, almost anytime a 7th chord comes up in a country song, you can use the matching Mixolydian mode over that chord. Also, many country songs sound good when you play Mixolydian over a straight major chord. Check out Brent Mason's playing on "Don't Rock the Jukebox" by Alan Jackson. The last note of the song ends on an F note, which is the ♭7th over a straight G major chord.

Almost anything in a chicken-pickin' style has a Mixolydian flavor to it. Learn to trust your ears. You don't want to sound too scalar and completely obvious, as if to say, "Now I'm playing Mixolydian." The idea is to incorporate the major 3rd, ♭7th, and occasional ♭5th notes of each chord into everything else in your bag of tricks. Chicken pickin', pentatonics, string bending, hybrid picking, etc. can all work together for a very funky texture with dominant 7th Mixolydian sounds.

"Workin' Man Blues" by Merle Haggard, "Liza Jane" by Vince Gill, or the southern rock Skynard classic "Sweet Home Alabama" are examples of songs using Mixolydian sounds.

Mixo-man

This solo uses a series of Mixolydian modes, as well as other country techniques and sounds. As each new 7th chord is played, the licks are based off that particular chord's Mixolydian mode. The solo's played with a pick, but some of it could be performed with hybrid picking. Note the quintuplets in bar 10—a good way to add a little rhythmic flash to your playing.

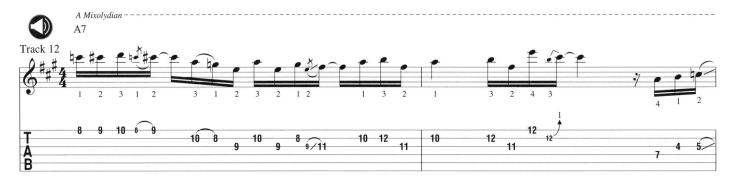

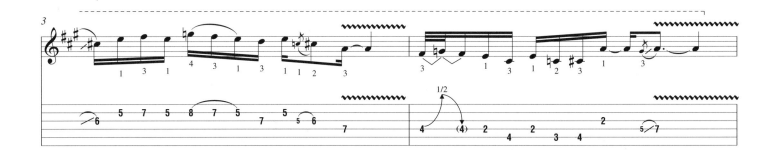

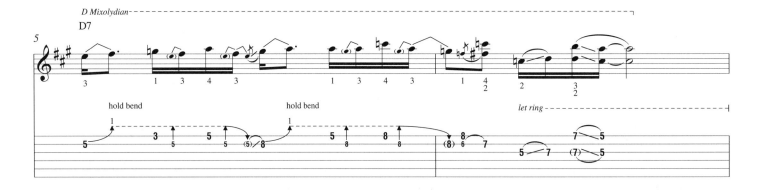

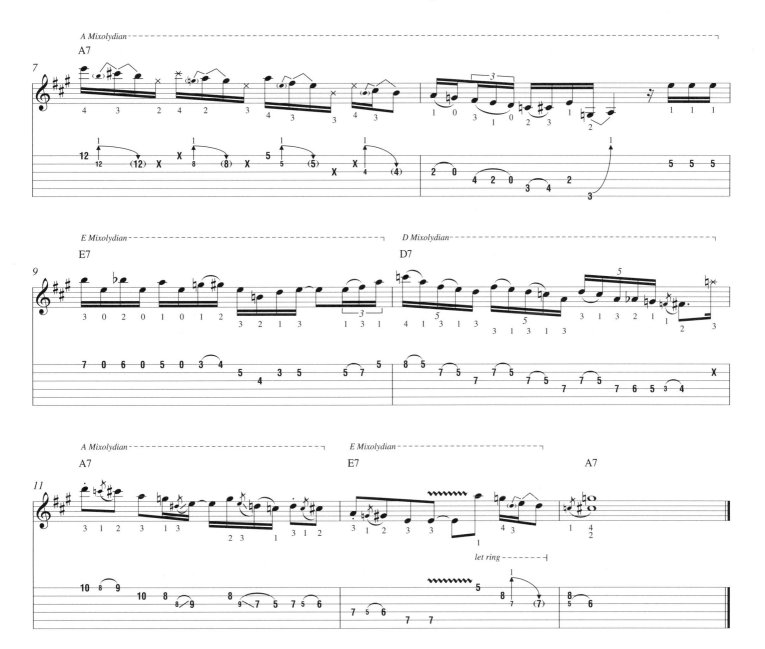

How to Use Minor Scales

Although not as common as major-key songs, there are plenty of minor-tonality country tunes—"Ghost Riders in the Sky," "Jolene," "Seminole Wind," and "Past the Point of Rescue," to name a few. If you were to play a solo on "House of the Rising Sun," you could technically use all of the minor scales presented in this book.

In country music, you have three basic minor tonalities to go along with your minor pentatonic scales: natural minor, Dorian, and harmonic minor. If you want to take your playing up to the next level, learn your minor scale patterns and how to use them properly. Then, as always, listen to some minor tunes, learn a few licks, and analyze what you are doing.

The easiest way to play over any minor song is to use only the tonic minor pentatonic scale, as discussed in the previous chapter. This will sound good, but if that's all you ever do, your playing will start to sound predictable and a little pedestrian. The chords of the song will determine what other minor scale you should use. You need to look for indicator chords in the chord progression that define what scale you should use. It's also very common in minor-key songs to use all the minor scales in one song (and sometimes even over just a couple of bars). As one note changes in the minor scale, its whole sound and function changes.

Natural Minor

The A natural minor scale is composed of A–B–C–D–E–F–G (it's the relative minor scale of C major). The indicator chords for natural minor, besides the i chord, are a minor iv chord (which would be a diatonic D minor) or a major ♭VI chord (a diatonic F major).

The A natural minor scale would work for all of these chords. The G chord is not an indicator chord because it could also work in A Dorian.

Dorian

The A Dorian mode has one note different from A natural minor: a major 6th, F♯, instead of an F. So, it's spelled: A–B–C–D–E–F♯–G. The big indicator chord for Dorian is a major or dominant IV chord. A D9 chord would function the same as a D7. The F♯ note in the scale is the major 3rd of the D7 chord.

Harmonic Minor

The A harmonic minor scale also has only one different note from the natural minor scale. It has a major 7th, G♯, as opposed to a G♮. It's spelled: A–B–C–D–E–F–G♯. Harmonic minor can be used when the song has a major or dominant V chord. That is your indicator chord. The G♯ note in the A harmonic minor scale is the major 3rd of an E or E7 chord.

Make sure you use the A harmonic minor scale and not the E harmonic minor scale. The dominant 7th V chord produces a very strong leading tone. Typically, this chord may last only one bar, or even just a couple of beats, but will sound really good if you nail it.

Minor Chord Progression

This progression in the key of D minor would use all three types of minor scales. You could also use D minor pentatonic at any time.

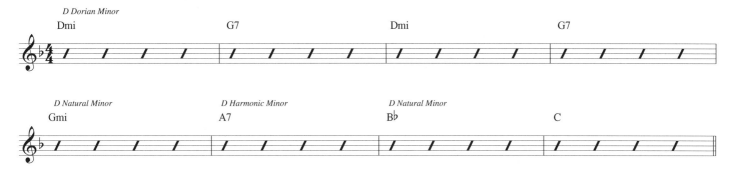

G7 is the dominant IV chord, which is the indicator chord for Dorian. Gmi is the minor iv chord, which is an indicator chord for natural minor. A7 is the dominant V chord, which is the indicator for harmonic minor. B♭ is the ♭VI major chord, which is an indicator for natural minor. The C chord (♭VII) also works in natural minor or Dorian.

Modal Interchange

A common example of *modal interchange* (or modal mixture) happens when you are in a major key and move to the *parallel minor*. In the following C major progression, a C natural minor scale would be used on the non-diatonic E♭ (♭III) chord. This is because the E♭ chord is "borrowed" from the parallel key of C minor. As opposed to relative keys, which use the same notes but have different tonics, parallel keys share the same tonic but use different notes. So, C major and A minor are relative keys, but C major and C minor are parallel keys.

Here's another example of modal interchange this time in the key of G major. You would switch to G minor on the minor iv chord, Cmi.

Minor Incident

This modern country solo gives a little taste of all the minor tonality scales presented in the book: natural minor, Dorian, harmonic minor, minor pentatonic, and a few added ♭5th notes, which usually work well when trying to add a blues flavor. This one also makes use are some Mark Knopfler-influenced chord-tone ideas, along with various other country guitar techniques and bends, which will be covered in upcoming chapters. When you're using a certain scale or arpeggio, try not to make it sound too deliberate or obvious. It should always sound like music, not a scale exercise.

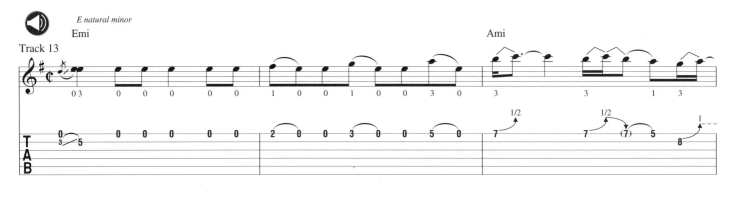

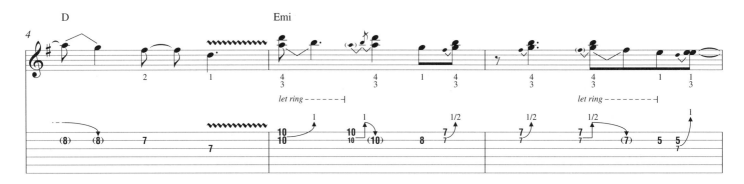

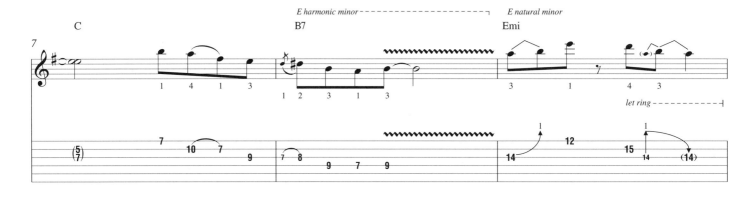

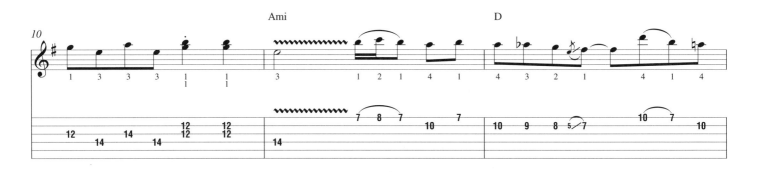

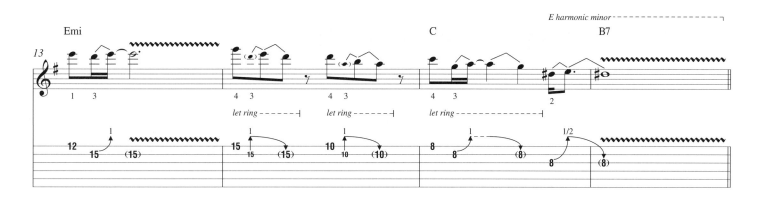

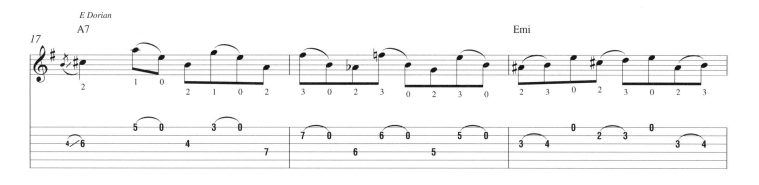

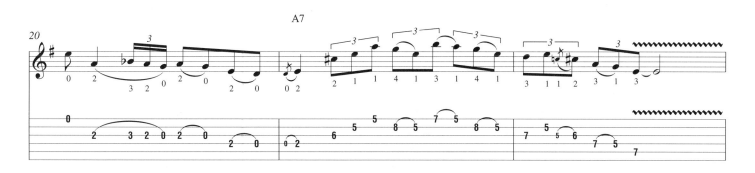

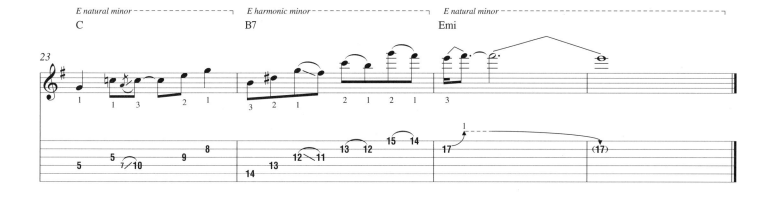

Chapter Three: String Bending

3

String bending is an integral part of modern country guitar playing and can be used to produce many uniquely country-sounding ideas. Everything from simple melodies and funky chicken pickin' to legato steel guitar sounds can be played using a variety of bends.

A country bend sounds different than a blues or rock bend. It tends to be a little more precise, slightly less aggressive, and at times a little stiffer-sounding. It helps to think of imitating a steel guitar, which achieves its note-bending with various mechanisms (pedals and levers), allowing a greater deal of precision with relatively little effort. Also, many country bends are played without vibrato or with a more controlled vibrato than in blues or rock, although in some of the rockin' modern country music, the bends are played with a rock attitude, sound, and vibrato.

Intonation and knowing which notes to bend to and from are two essential elements of country bending. Generally speaking, bending or release-bending to a chord tone is your best choice. Bending to melody notes or scale tones that are not actual chord tones can also sound good. Whole-step and half-step bends are most often used, but quarter-step bends and minor 3rd bends can be used in the right contexts, as well.

Notes can be bent on all strings, and all four fingers on your left hand can be used. If the strings on your guitar are difficult to bend, try using a lighter-gauge string. A set of .009s is a good place to start. Both regular flatpicking and hybrid picking can be used.

Supportive Fingering

When bending a note, try to use more than one finger whenever possible to increase your strength and to get a better grip on the string. If you're bending with your third finger, for example, try placing your first and second finger on the same string, directly behind the third, and then bend up using the strength of all three fingers. When bending with your second finger, you only have your first available for support. Some situations will not allow you to use supportive fingering, but with practice, your hands get stronger and the bending gets easier. Don't be afraid to wrap your thumb around the top edge of your guitar neck for extra support if necessary.

Intonation

Bending a note in tune to a specific targeted note is the most important element of a good country bend. Different areas of the guitar neck and different strings require varying amounts of pressure to achieve the desired bend. Use your ears and strive to keep each bend in tune. Double-check yourself by playing the targeted note as a normal fretted note before bending up to it.

Bending Licks

Let's check out some of these various bend techniques with a few licks.

1. Whole-step Bend

This lick demonstrates whole-step bends. A whole step is two frets on the guitar.

2. Half-step Bend

Here's a half-step bending lick. A half step is one fret on the guitar. This bend requires much less pressure than a whole-step bend.

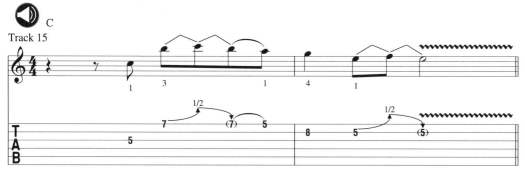

3. Quarter-step Bend

In some cases, a note will be bent a quarter step and never accurately hit a target note on purpose. This produces a bluesy effect; as long as you're in control, this can sound great.

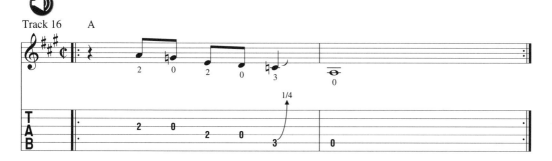

4. Pre-bends and Release Bends

A *release bend* is when a note is pre-bent up to a targeted note, picked, and then released until the note becomes a normal fretted note. Make sure that the note keeps ringing as it's being released.

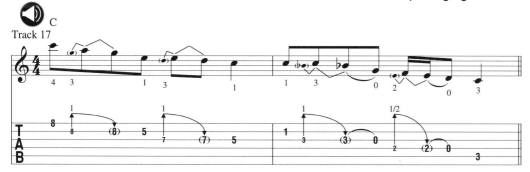

5. Bend-and-Hold

Bend a note up—usually on the second or third string—and then hold the bend as you play notes on higher strings. You would then usually pick the original bent note again and release it. This technique is very common in steel guitar licks.

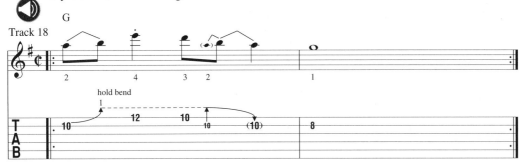

6. Vibrato

A good-sounding vibrato on some of your bent notes can add a lot of character when used properly. Even though many country bends will not use vibrato, having this technique down will give you more control in general. On a bent note, the vibrato seems to come from a combination of your wrist moving back and forth and a little finger movement. A good vibrato should be deep and solid and not sound like a fast quiver. It may take some time to develop.

7. Fast Vibrato

Sometimes a fast vibrato can sound good for an old-school steel guitar effect.

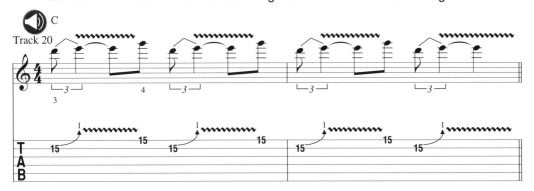

Out on a Bender

This tune combines most of the aspects of country-style string-bending. There are notes bent on all six strings, half- and whole-step bends, release bends, bend-and-hold moves, and bends combined with open strings. Always pay attention to the chord you are playing over. Look for the chord and scale tones and how that particular bend relates to that chord. Strive for good intonation, use supportive fingering where possible, and try to make everything sound smooth and seamless.

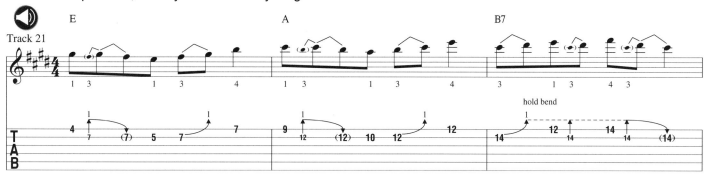

Track 21

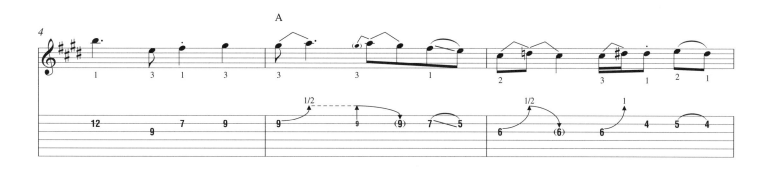

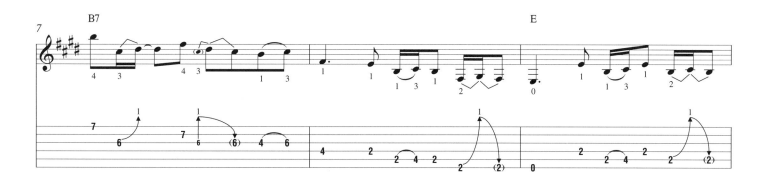

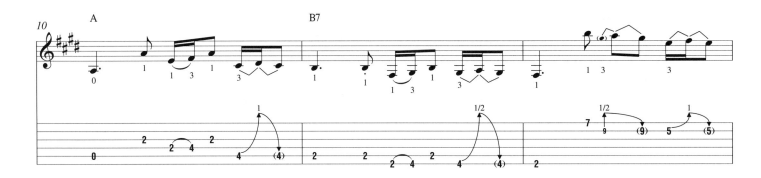

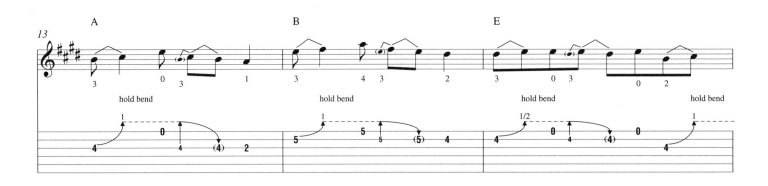

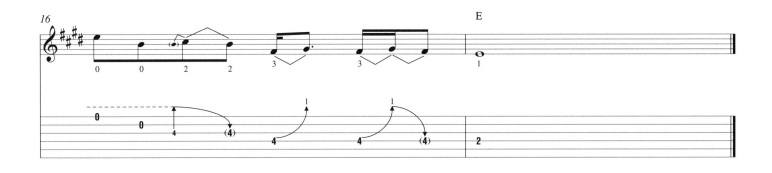

Chapter Four:
4 Hybrid Picking

Hybrid picking is a technique used by most of today's country guitar players. It involves using a flatpick along with your middle finger and/or ring finger. Many players use a thumbpick along with their index and middle fingers for the same effect. This technique can be used for many uniquely country-sounding ideas.

Some players use fingernails or fake fingernails on their right hand, while others use bare fingers. Fingernails will give you a brighter sound; bare fingers give you more "thunk." Experiment to find what works best for you.

To add a chicken-pickin' flavor to your guitar playing, pluck the string with your finger and let it slap against the fretboard, producing a sharp, short, accented note. The contrast in tone between the flatpicked notes and the fingerpicked ones results in a distinctive country pickin' sound. We'll talk more on this in the next chapter.

The concept of hybrid picking is also useful for playing banjo-type rolls, steel guitar licks, and other uniquely country-sounding ideas. Virtually every contemporary country guitar player uses a version of this style for soloing and rhythm playing.

Pick-It Fence

This tune features a Merle Travis-type hybrid-picking rhythm pattern, which can be used in many country songs. It's played here in a rockabilly style, with a few licks thrown in-between the chord changes. It's important to play the alternating bass notes with your pick and the high strings with your fingers. Rest your right palm on the bridge for a muted-bass-note effect, as this will help with the separation of the parts.

To learn this tune, concentrate on the first four bars until the picking feels natural; then try playing the rest of the tune. Play it very slowly at first and speed up as you become more comfortable.

Track 22

Hybrid Rockin' Rhythm

This example demonstrates how hybrid picking can be used to create a funky-sounding rockin' rhythm pattern. All the double stops are played with your fingers, while the lower notes are played with your pick. Play agressively to make the notes pop.

Track 23

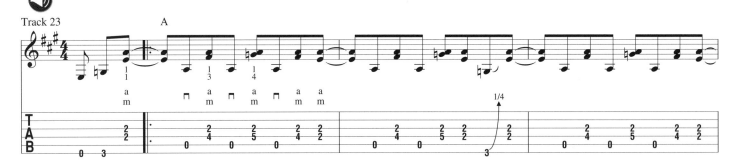

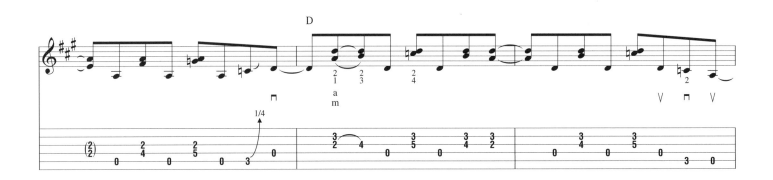

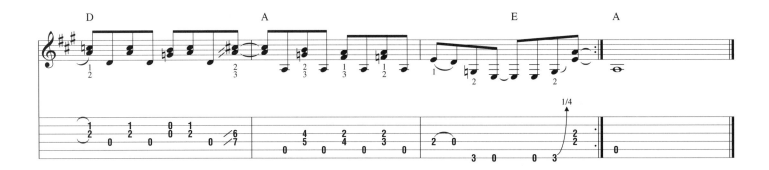

Rolling on a G String

This tune is an exercise designed to get your pick and fingers working together in a banjo rolling motion. The same picking pattern continues throughout the chord progression. Speed it up when you can play it smoothly without mistakes.

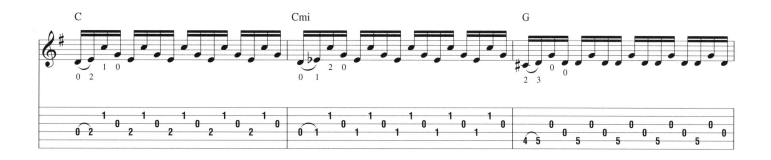

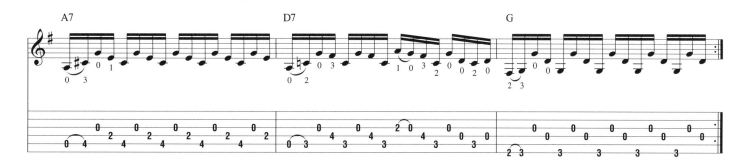

Pick-and-Roll

Pick-and-roll is a hybrid picking technique whereby you pick a lower note with the pick and then pluck the next two strings in a rolling motion with your middle and ring fingers, similar to what a banjo player or a steel guitarist would play. Using triads and three-note chord forms, you pick-and-roll through the notes in an upward or downward motion lengthwise on the guitar neck. You can create some some nice, fast, and fluid licks using the technique, as well as some great chicken-pickin' effects.

Pick-and-Roll #1

To demonstrate this technique, this example picks and rolls through an E minor triad. It starts with an open Emi chord and then uses various Emi triads to move up the neck. As with most pick-and-roll licks, use your pick for the lowest note and your middle and ring finger for the next two strings.

Pick-and-Roll #2

This idea works for an A7 sound. The triplets work well over a shuffle rhythm. A B note, which is the 9th of an A7 chord, is added for a more complex sound. In the second bar, the chord shape moves up chromatically and then resolves to an A triad in 12th position. Try playing the second bar staccato (as notated) for a chicken-pickin' effect. This is acheived by letting up on each note a little with your left hand.

Track 26

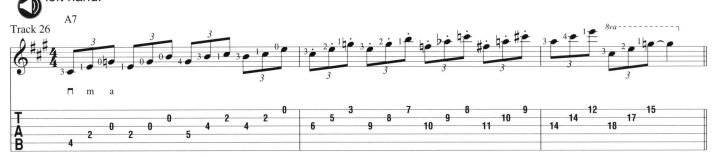

Pick-and-Roll #3

This pick-and-roll lick in G major moves up the neck and ends with a D triad resolving to G. Also try it with a triplet rhythm. Let the notes ring, and then play it staccato for a chicken-pickin' sound.

Track 27

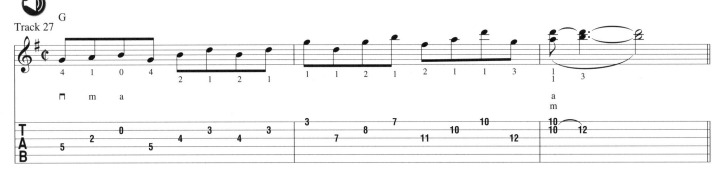

Pick-and-Roll #4

This roll is similar to Chet Atkins' version of "Orange Blossom Special." The same right-hand pattern is used throughout.

Track 28

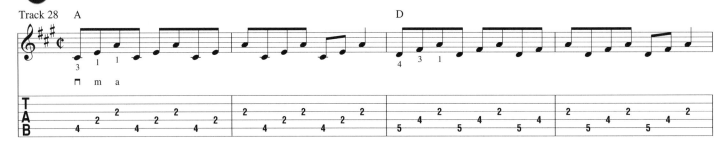

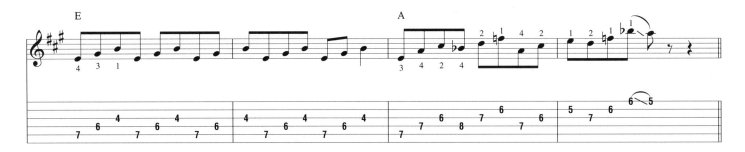

Staccato 6ths

This example of the pick-and-roll creates a chicken-pickin' sound using 6th intervals. Play the notes staccato while muting the note on the second string with your left hand's middle finger.

Staccato 6ths #1

A triplet will work perfectly on a shuffle groove. It will also work well over a straight-eighth or two-beat feel but will create some rhythmic tension, which can be used very effectively to add another interesting dimension to your playing. The right-hand picking pattern remains constant.

Track 29

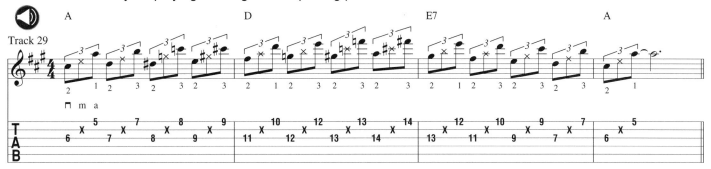

Staccato 6ths #2

Here's the same type of lick but played with eighth notes over a two-beat feel. The accent shifts with each new 6th interval. You're also not limited to the first three strings. This example makes use of strings 5–1.

Track 30

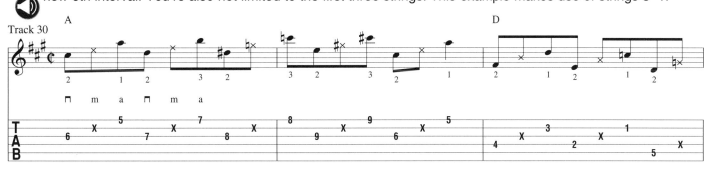

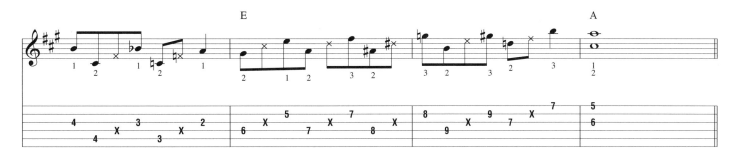

Staccato 6ths #3

This next example uses a technique I call *rapid-fire triplets*. Using the pick-and-roll technique, you play the notes similarly to the previous example, muting the second string with your middle finger, but you also add one more picked note on the third string.

Track 31

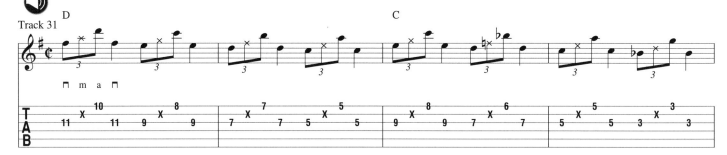

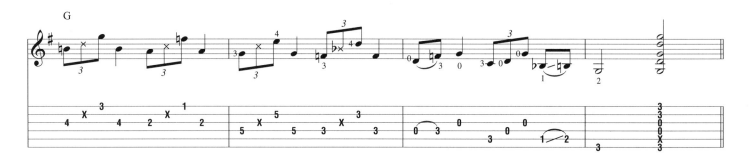

Chapter Five:
5 Chicken Pickin'

Chicken pickin' is the style many people associate with country guitar. It combines various country techniques and uses a lot of funkier, blues-type sounds combined with your basic pentatonic scales, chromatic notes, string bending, steel guitar licks, double stops, and percussive clucking accents. Basically, you can throw in the kitchen sink if you'd like.

Made popular by players like James Burton, Albert Lee, Roy Nichols, and, more recently, Brent Mason and Brad Paisley, it's usually played with some form of hybrid picking and a little left-hand muting to create a plucking sound from the strings that, at times can sound like a clucking chicken. You can also get these percussive accents by using only your pick and left-hand muting.

To demonstrate basic chicken-pickin' technique, first play this blues lick with your pick and a distorted tone.

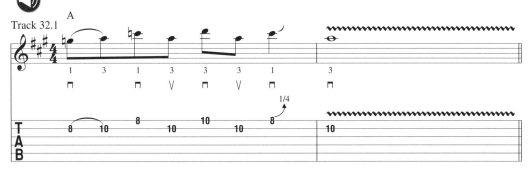

Now clean up your sound and try the same lick with hybrid picking and a little muting on your left hand, trying to make the notes cluck. For the muted notes, lift up the finger on your left hand as you pick it. You can also get the effect by just using your pick and playing the notes staccato, but you get a little more plucking sound by using your pick and fingers. Experiment with some other licks you know.

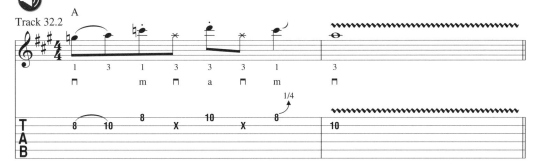

Chicken Pickin' Licks

Now let's hear the technique in action.

Chicken Pickin' #1

This is your basic Chet Atkins chicken sound. Mute with your left hand for the staccato effect. Use this lick for your job interview at KFC.

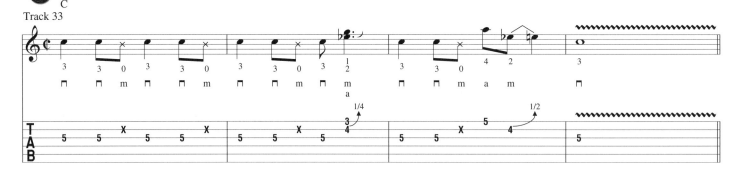

Chicken Pickin' #2

Try moving this classic lick over different chords; it's a very useable lick. Note the fourth note, B, which is muted by lifting the finger on your left hand.

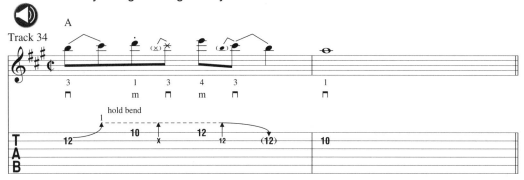

Chicken Pickin' #3

In this Roy Nichols-style example, the note on the second string is struck with the pick and then the fingers, which creates a stuttering effect. Hold the bend on the second string but release it gradually.

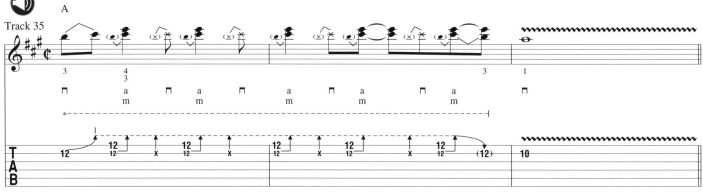

*hold bend & gradually release

Chicken Pickin' #4

This lick makes use of some double stops.

Track 36

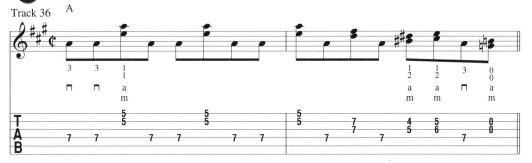

Chicken Pickin' #5

Some 6ths can be used quite effectively for some classic chicken-pickin' sounds.

Track 37

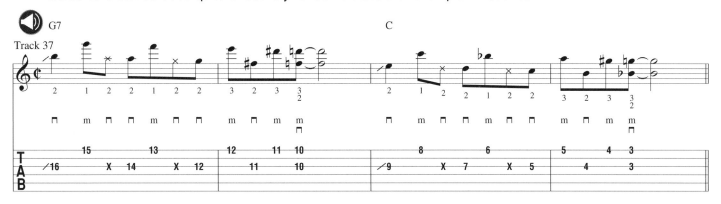

Chicken Pickin' #6

Here's a similar lick using 6ths with a rapid-fire triplet picking pattern. Your second finger on the left hand mutes the second string. Use hybrid picking or try it with your pick only, sweeping the triplet with a downstroke and picking the quarter notes with an upstroke.

Track 38

Chicken Pickin' #7

This lick makes use of first-finger bends for a plucky D7 sound.

Track 39

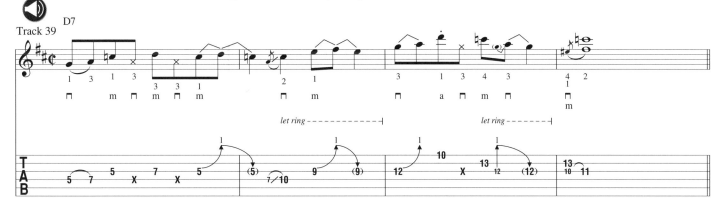

Chicken Pickin' #8

Pay close attention to the right-hand picking and left-hand fingering to achieve the right effect. When playing at a fast tempo, you can grace over the triplets by playing them very staccato.

Track 40

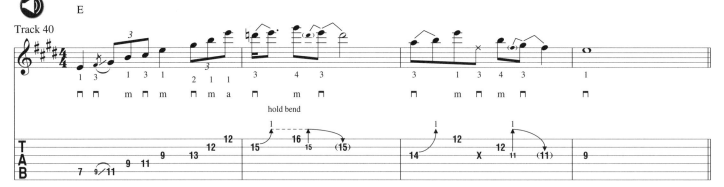

Chicken Pickin' #9

This hot lick uses triplets, which add rhythmic tension, along with pull-offs, open strings, and a funky double stop at the end. Pay close attention to the fingering and the third-finger slide in the last bar.

Track 41

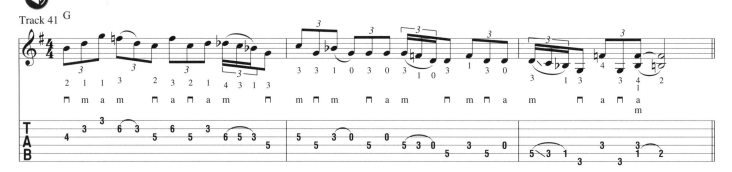

Chicken Pickin' #10

Here's a chicken-pickin' lick using just your pick and left-hand muting to get a clucking sound. To play the rake, mute the open strings with your right palm as you sweep with a downstroke.

Track 42.1

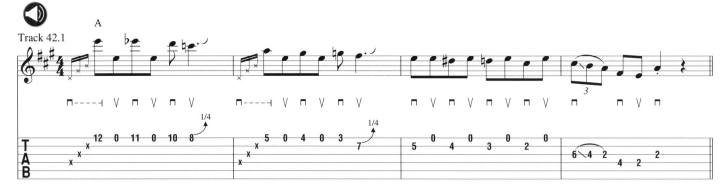

Chicken Pickin' #11

Here's a Bakersfield-style lick in E.

Track 42.2

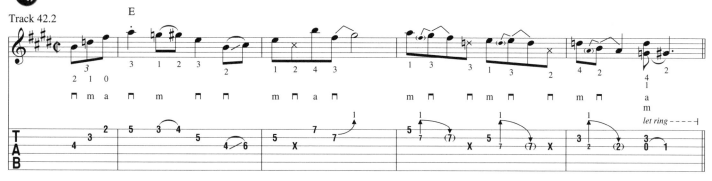

Poultry in Motion

This solo uses a variety of chicken-pickin' licks. Learn each lick individually—slowly at first—and then learn to play them together as a cohesive solo. Also experiment with hybrid picking as notated or getting a chicken-pickin' sound flatpicking. For example, in bars 9–10, try using the pick only with sweeping downward for each arpeggio. Make sure you do a lot of muting with your left hand to help the clucking, stuttering sound that makes this style work.

Track 43

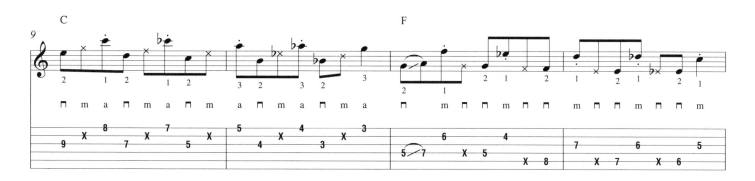

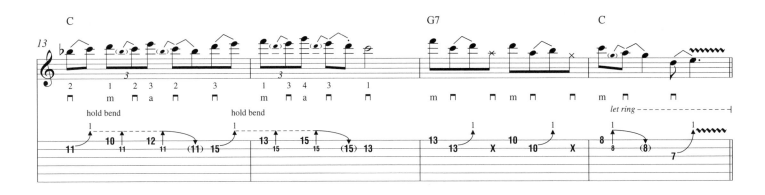

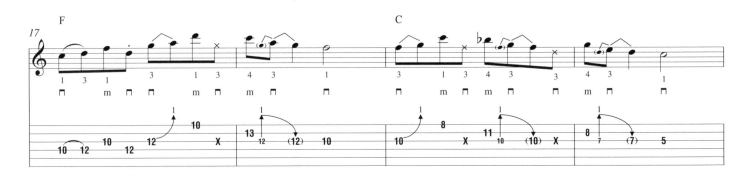

D.C. al Coda

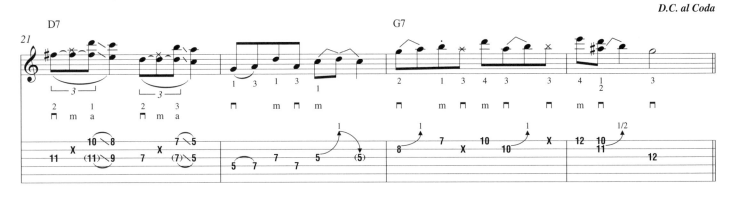

⊕ **Coda**

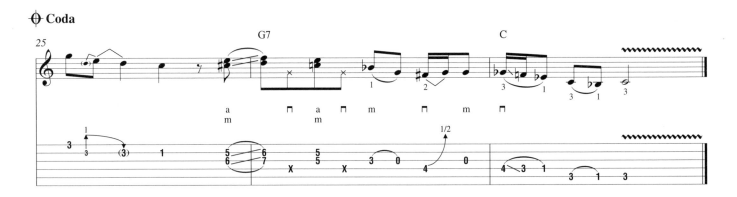

Chapter Six:
6 Flatpicking

Flatpicking is a style of guitar in which the notes are played with a regular pick and combined with some hammer-ons and pull-offs on the left hand. It generally refers to bluegrass-style guitar playing on acoustic guitar and often takes place in open position. Flatpicking could be considered the opposite of fingerstyle or hybrid picking. Bluegrass players all flatpick because you get a clear, even, powerful tone that enables an acoustic guitar to cut through and be heard in a band situation. On electric guitar, flatpicking also produces a clean, even sound that has advantages. With good flatpicking technique, you can learn to play some very fast, impressive-sounding country licks and keep up with the hot fiddle player!

Blending bluegrass-style flatpicking with traditional country and rock 'n' roll guitar licks gives you the sound you hear on many modern country recordings. The key to good flatpicking is to develop good technique and dexterity in both of your hands and have a good working knowledge of your scales in open position, as well as other positions up the neck. Most of the licks are based off of open chord and triad shapes or some form of sequenced scale pattern. Chromatic notes and dissonance can be used to great effect, as well.

Use alternate picking for speed and precision, although sweeping and other techniques are appropriate at times. As a general rule, any note on a downbeat should be picked with a downstroke, but there are exceptions.

Flatpicking Licks
These phrases will give you a good idea of what this technique is all about.

Flatpicking #1
This is the grandaddy of all famous bluegrass licks and is based on an open G chord. If you learn nothing else from this book, learn this lick!

Track 44 G

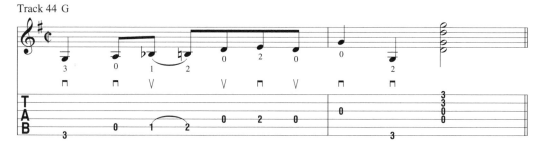

Flatpicking #2
Here's a variation of the same lick, based on a open C chord.

Track 45
C

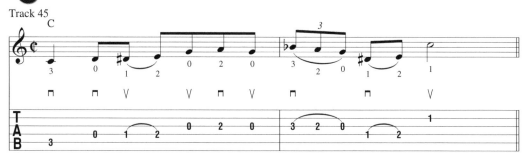

Flatpicking #3

This lick uses sequencing in the key of D major. Note the open strings in bars 3 and 4. You could also fret those two notes when moving this lick to a different key.

Track 46

Flatpicking #4

This idea combines scale sequencing with chromatic notes for an E7 sound. Use alternate picking, or you could add more pull-offs, as well.

Track 47

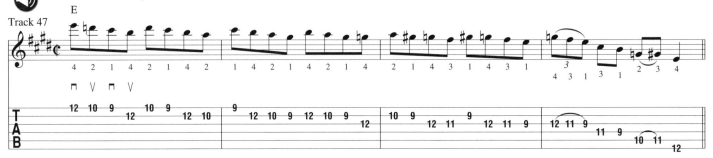

Flatpicking #5

Pay close attention to the picking on this lick in the key of A. Note the pull-off to the open E string in the second bar. This phrase could work well as a nice ending lick.

Track 48

Flatpicking #6

This one takes place in an open G chord position and uses a series of pull-offs.

Track 49

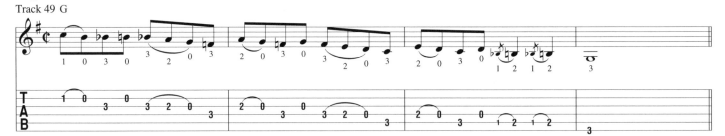

Flat Tire Blues

This flatpicking solo uses all of the techniques we've talked about and a few more not mentioned. Pay close attention to the chords being played over and how the licks concentrate on the chord tones. Use alternate picking whenever possible. At bars 22–25, try sweeping through the chord shapes while letting the notes ring into each other. This tune also demonstrates the use of chromaticism, which was discussed earlier in the book.

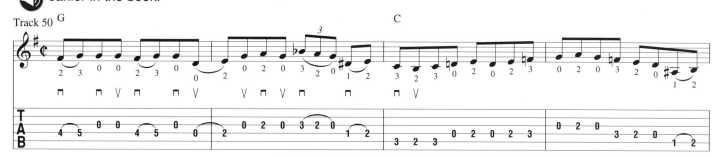

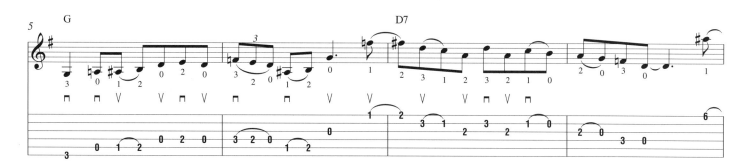

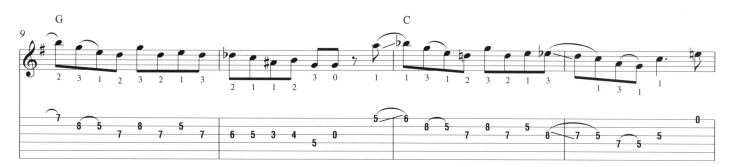

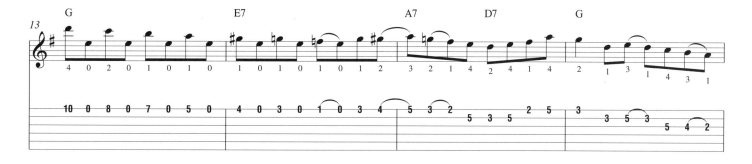

Chapter Seven:
7 Pickin' on the Low Strings

Country pickers use the low strings for a lot of different parts. Walk-ups and walk-downs are very common, as are melodic solos, low tremolo melodies, rhythm parts, bent notes, drop D tuning riffs, and anything else that you can think of (check out Chapter 9 for some really funky-sounding double stops on the low strings). So turn up the treble, use that bridge Tele pickup, and have at it!

Man in Black

This tune is played in the style of Luther Perkins, the legendary guitarist for Johnny Cash. His rhythm style using the lower strings on the guitar was a signature driving force behind Johnny's unique sound on songs like "Folsom Prison Blues" and "Ring of Fire." This technique can be used on many country tunes to drive the local yokel Cash fans wild! Mute the low strings with the palm of your right hand on the bridge to create a rhythmic, percussive pattern effect as you pick the strings. Pay close attention to the muted notes and the picking pattern.

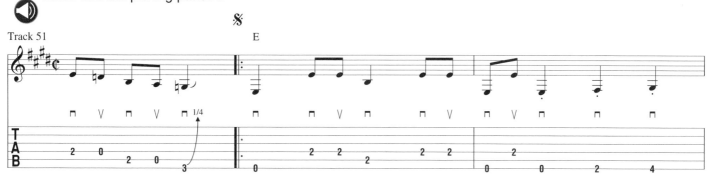

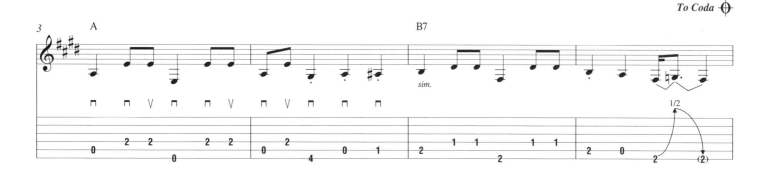

Chapter Eight:
8 Pedal Steel Guitar Sounds

What Is a Pedal Steel Guitar?

A *pedal steel guitar* is a stringed instrument usually with 10 strings and no frets. It sits flat on a stand and is played with a steel bar as a slide, along with a thumbpick and steel fingerpicks on the picking hand. Different tunings are used, but the two most common are open E9 and C6. Many players use a double-neck steel, with each neck using a separate tuning. Under the guitar are a series of pedals and knee levers that bend certain strings up a half step or a whole step, enabling the player to hit notes that would not be available with just the straight bar.

The sound that this instrument produces can be very legato and haunting as the notes slide, bend, and weave through a chord progression. It can also be played at very quick tempos with rapid-fire licks and banjo-type rolls. Chord melodies also sound unique on a steel guitar. Many players use the C6 neck to play close-voiced chord clusters prevalent in a lot of cow jazz and Western swing music.

Pedal Steel Emulation on Guitar

Country guitar players love to transcribe these traditional country-sounding ideas to regular six-string guitar. Most guitar players have a catalog of steel-guitar-sounding ideas that they can draw from. Many times, it's easier to transcribe these ideas than those of a steel guitar player, which sometimes can be near impossible to play on a regular guitar. But keep in mind that it's the sound and feel you are looking for—not necessarily an exact replica. Some country guitar players use a device called a B-string bender, which gives you a few different bending options.

One of the main things that make a steel guitar sound unique is that one or more notes will sustain as another note bends. Developing this technique on guitar will force you to use some unfamiliar fingerings that are hard to grab. Try using supportive fingering when possible. Also try adding a little compression and reverb to your sound to smooth out the rough edges. A volume pedal can also be used to ease up or eliminate the attack on a note, which can help to enhance the pedal-steel effect, as it's very common on that instrument.

All the ideas and chord theory related to scales, double stops, and triads discussed in this book apply to steel guitar licks. Experiment with different right-hand picking options using your fingers, hybrid picking, or straight flatpicking. Generally speaking, however, hybrid picking is most commonly used when emulating the steel guitar.

Buddy Emmons, Tom Brumley, Paul Franklin, Gary Morse, Wally Murphy, Sonny Garrish, Dan Dugmore, Jay Dee Maness, Greg Liesz, Marty Rifkin, and many more can be heard playing pedal steel guitar on many of country music's top recordings. Guitarists like James Burton, Albert Lee, Brent Mason, Red Volkaert, Jerry Donahue, Pete Anderson, and Brad Paisley can be heard bending guitar strings to imitate the pedal steel.

Basic Bends and Sounds

To learn to play steel guitar licks, we'll first learn some basic bends to fit major, minor, and dominant 7th chord sounds. The best-sounding bends usually end on a chord tone.

The idea is to take a basic bend and then change the phrasing, picking pattern, or even add a note or two to create some steel-sounding licks and melodies. Your pick alone and the hybrid picking techinque can both be used for good effect.

Major Sounds

Examples 1–5 are based off a C major barre chord at the eighth fret. Remember, the idea is to bend up to or release a bend to a chord tone as you hold another note or two. Examples 6–8 are based off a fifth-string-root C barre chord at the third fret. Example 9 is based off a C triad at the 12th fret. Examples 10–13 are first-finger bends that are difficult at first but get easier with practice.

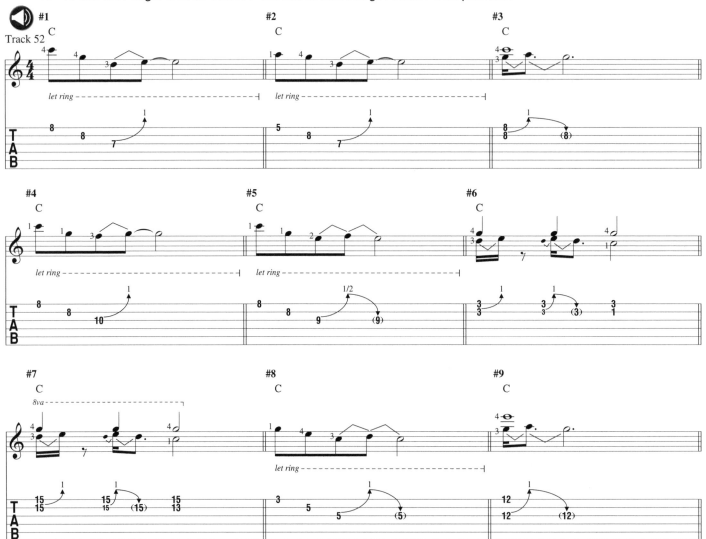

Chapter Eight: Pedal Steel Guitar Sounds

Bending with your first finger allows the lower note to remain static. It takes a little practice but sounds very good.

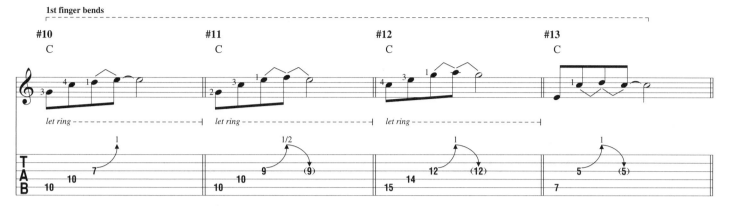

Minor Sounds

The difference between a minor chord and a major chord is that the 3rd is a half step lower in minor. This causes the chord to sound dark and moody. Many major bends can be turned into minor by reducing a bend up to the 3rd by a half step. For example, in the key of C, for a major sound you would bend a D note up to E, but for a minor sound, bend the D note up to E♭. All other elements of a major or dominant 7th chord would remain the same. A ♭7th note works well in minor or dominant. In the key of C, the ♭7th is B♭. Be very careful when turning a major bend into a minor bend, as it is very easy to over-bend the note.

This example shows how to turn a major bend into a minor one.

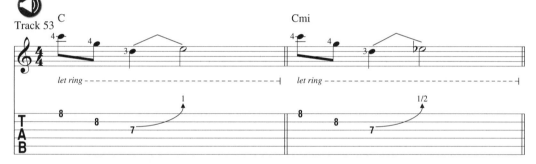

It's also important to note that C minor is the relative minor of E♭ major. So most E♭ major licks will work well for C minor. You may need to hear a bass note beneath the chord to hear the difference between the major and minor tonalities.

The following example illustrates the exact same bend as E♭ major and C minor by using different bass notes.

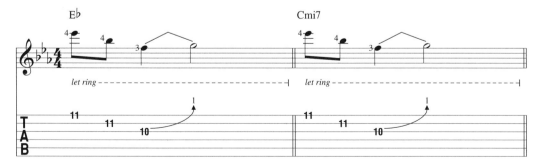

These three examples use the same fingering at different places on the neck for three C minor sounds. Note that #3 is a half-step bend.

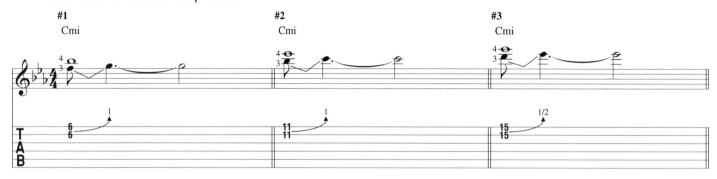

First-finger bends are used in examples 5–7. Note that #7 is an A Dorian sound.

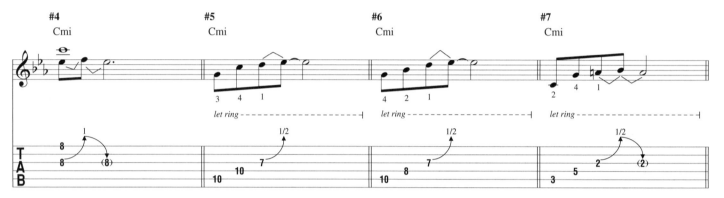

Dominant 7th Sounds

Adding a ♭7th note to a major triad gives you a dominant 7th chord. In the key of C, the ♭7th is B♭. In many situations, a dominant 7th sound can be used over a straight major chord for a funky, bluesy tonality.

Track 54

Getting Bent

This example shows how to take a basic steel guitar idea—in this case, major sound #1—and morph it into different licks by following the chords and varying the notes and phrasing.

8

Steel Guitar Licks

Here are a few examples of some classic-sounding steel guitar ideas using the basic bends as a starting point. For a lot of these licks, you have to use hybrid picking to avoid hitting unwanted strings.

Steel Guitar #1

This is a funky A major steel lick. Note the G♮ note, which is the ♭7th.

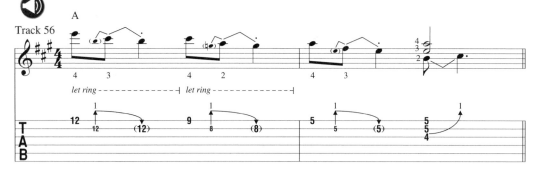

Steel Guitar #2

This lick imitates the sound of a steel guitar player pressing and releasing a pedal to bend the A note to B and back.

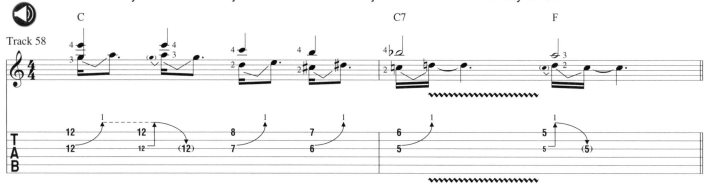

Steel Guitar #3

This lick takes you from a C major chord to C7 to F major—or I–I7–IV in the key of C.

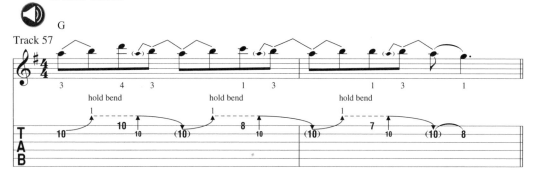

52

Steel Guitar #4

This lick starts out based off a G triad at the seventh fret and works through a few first-finger bends on C, D, and G chords.

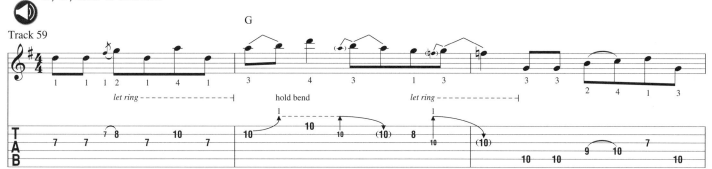

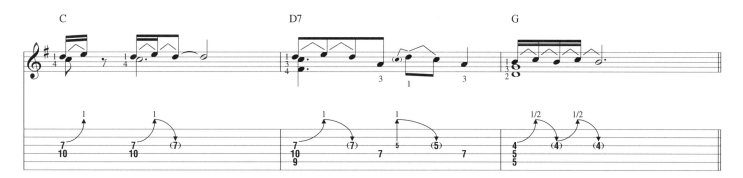

Steel Guitar #5

This steel guitar lick is a very usable walk-down from the V chord to the I chord. In this case, that's E7 to A using 6th intervals.

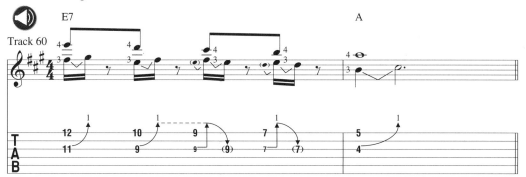

Steel Guitar #6

Here's a V–I walk-down idea going from G7 to C using 3rd intervals. The same lick could be used in the key of G as I–IV.

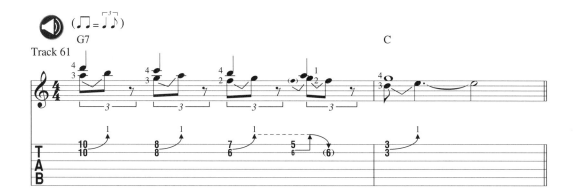

Steel Guitar #7

In this typical chord progression, similar fingerings are moved up the neck in the first four bars to define the different chord qualities. In bar 6, over the G7 chord, pay close attention to the fingering and the upstroke rake used on the first beat.

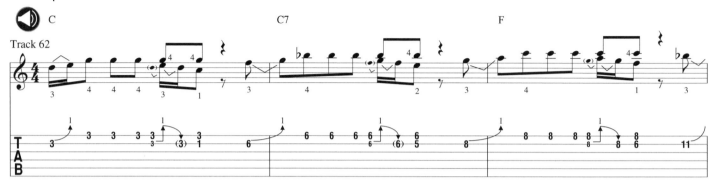

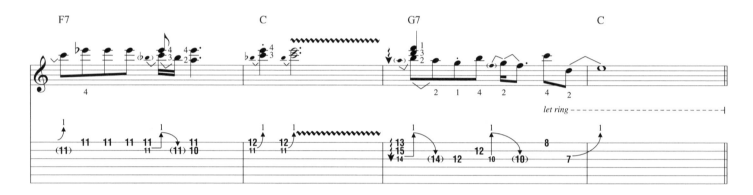

Steel Guitar #8

This example demonstrates steel licks over a fast two-beat tempo. Similar rhythms are used for each lick. Try flatpicking and hybrid picking for different textures.

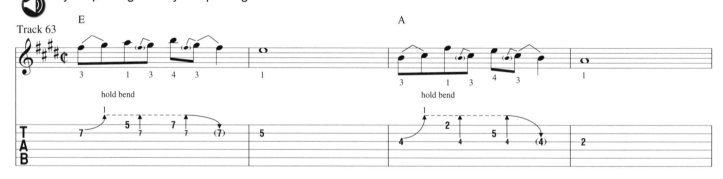

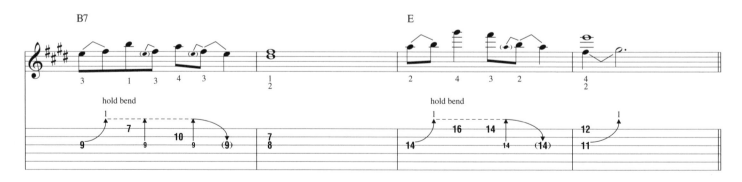

Steel Guitar #9

This legato steel lick works its way down the C major scale via a series of pre-bends and releases. Let the notes ring into each other as much as possible. Pay very close attention to intonation.

Track 64

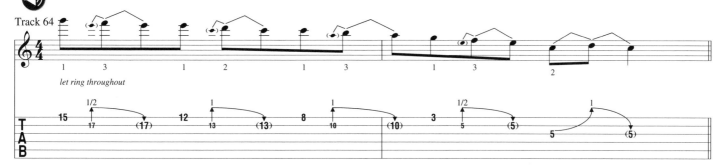

let ring throughout

Steel Guitar #10

This lick works its way down a diatonic A major scale via a series of first-finger bends. It starts with a C♯, the 3rd of A, on the bass note.

Track 65

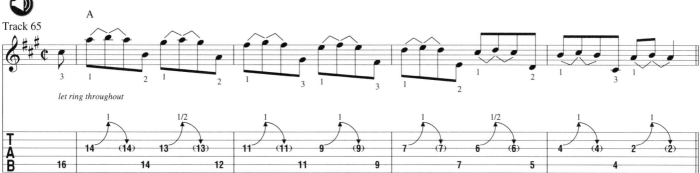

let ring throughout

Steel Guitar #11

Using the same basic lick but changing the G♯ notes to G natural gives you an A7 sound, which resolves nicely to D major.

Track 66

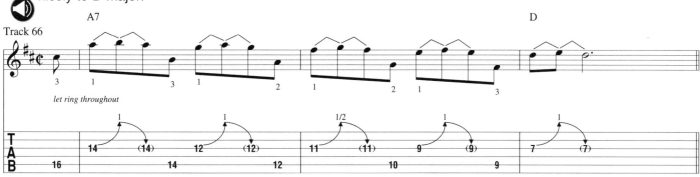

let ring throughout

Dixie Waltz

This tune is based on a standard country chord progression. It combines many aspects of steel guitar emulation. Strive for smoothness and good intonation. Use supportive fingering when possible. Try using a compressor pedal, some drippy reverb, and a quarter-note delay.

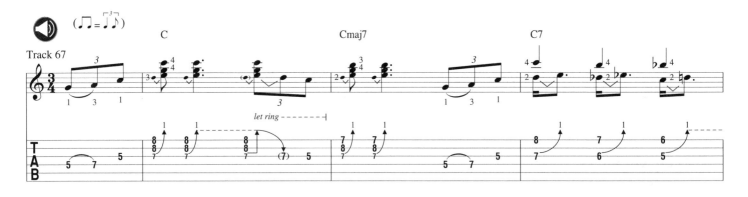
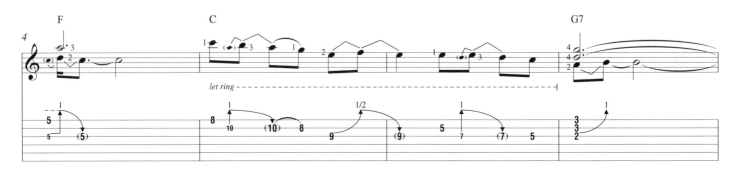
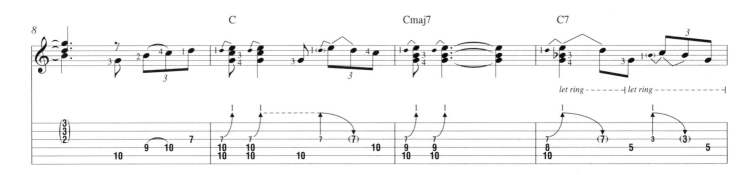

Chapter Nine: Double Stops

9

A *double stop* can be defined as playing two notes at the same time, in harmony with each other. This technique is used to give melodies a fuller sound, to spice up single-note lines, and to add harmony to a musical phrase.

In country guitar, double stops can be played with your pick or accented with hybrid picking to add a percussive, funky texture to your playing. They can be very handy in all aspects of county guitar playing, including solos, rhythm parts, chords, and fills in-between vocal lines. The most common types of double stops are 3rds, 4ths, and 6ths.

To begin to understand how and where to use double stops, you should learn to harmonize major scales as double stops. Here is the C major scale in 3rds on the first two strings. It lays out well on the guitar because the C root is at the first fret of the second string.

This next example is in the key of A. Transpose this scale in 3rds to different keys so you become comfortable with all keys up and down the neck. Try starting on the root, go up as high as you can, and then come all the way down to the lowest possible fret, working back up to the root.

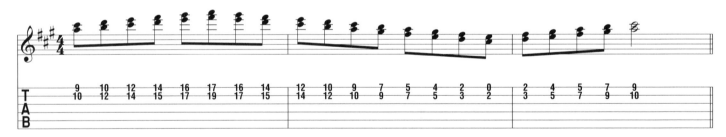

Practice the following examples in ascending and descending fashion and in as many different keys as possible. Try starting on the root, as well as the lowest possible fret. Eventually, you'll begin to see the scales instantaneously, making them easier to use. Now learn your scales in 3rds on all sets of strings, transposing them to as many keys as you can.

A good way to practice is to take a different key every day and play 3rds on all string sets.

A major on 2nd and 3rd strings   E major on 3rd and 4th strings   C major on 4th and 5th strings   G major on 5th and 6th strings

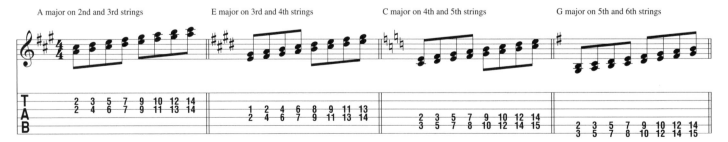

Chapter Nine: Double Stops

The 6th interval is also very commonly used in country guitar playing. Try hybrid picking, using the pick on the lower note and a finger for the higher note. Practice these scales in all keys and string combinations.

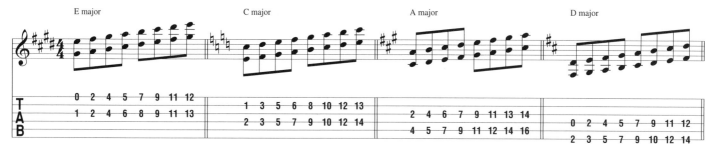

You should also play 3rds and 6th scales while staying in one position, using the five major scale patterns. Transpose to different keys and patterns.

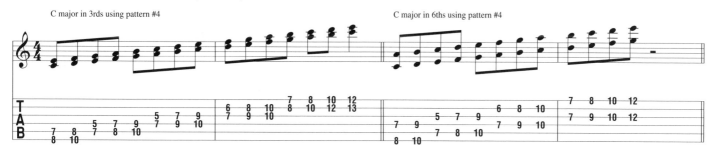

Leading to Chords

Playing lead guitar in a country band often requires the guitar player to "lead" the band through the chord changes. Using 3rds and 6ths in scalar movement sounds good for this purpose. This tune demonstrates this concept in a simple fashion.

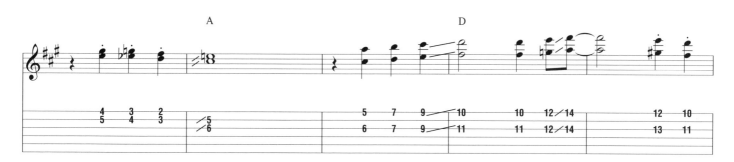

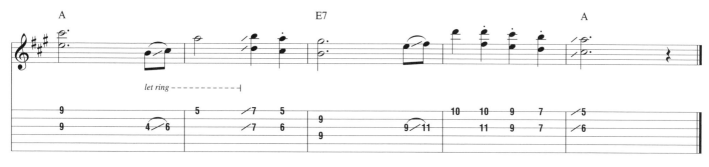

Using Pentatonic Scales for Double Stops

Pentatonic scales provide an easy way to play double stops with relative ease of fingering. The way the scales lay out on the guitar makes it easy to alternate between 3rds and 4ths for some interesting sounds. The idea presented here is to play a major pentatonic scale and use hammer-ons to get a double-stop sound. Playing like this also sounds a little like Floyd Kramer's piano style.

To demonstrate this technique, first play this extended C major pentatonic scale with the root on the fifth string.

Now, if you hammer onto the string from directly below each note, using only the notes from the scale, you get some good-sounding, easy-to-use double stops.

Track 69.1

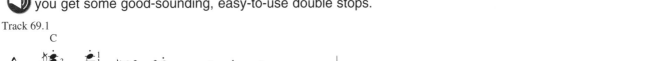

Here's an F major pentatonic pattern with hammer-ons.

Track 69.2 F

And here are a couple of licks using pentatonic hammer-ons.

Track 70.1

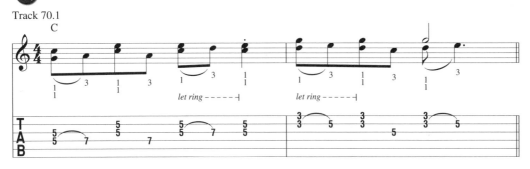

Track 70.2

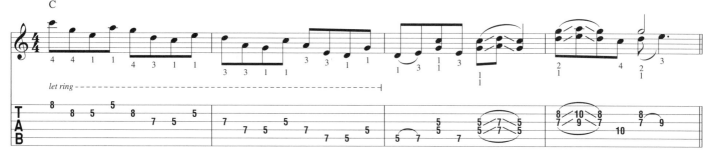

This lick uses a harmonized pentatonic scale. Let the notes in the first two bars ring into each other for a double-stop sound. Sliding 4ths, as in the last two bars, works well in the right situation.

Track 70.3

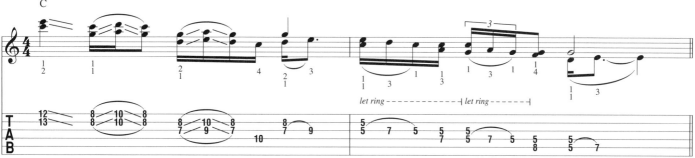

This lick combines 3rds and sliding 4ths with pentatonic hammer-ons.

Track 70.4

Double Dippin'

This solo uses all of the double-stop ideas mentioned: 3rds, 4ths, 6ths, hammer-ons, and slides are used to weave in and around this standard country chord progression. The hammer-ons give the tune a Floyd Kramer piano effect. As with the other solos in this book, always try and relate the notes and licks to the chords. That makes for solid, harmonically sound country guitar playing and is an extremely important factor with respect to taking your guitar work to the next level. It will also enable you to use the new ideas in different songs.

You can combine regular pick playing and hybrid picking on certain parts for effect.

Chapter Nine: Double Stops

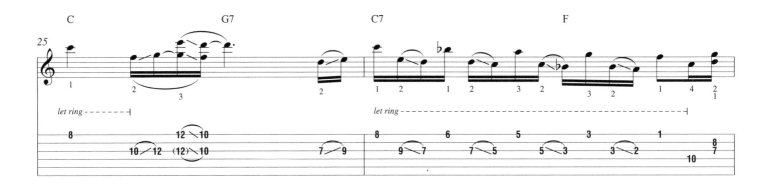

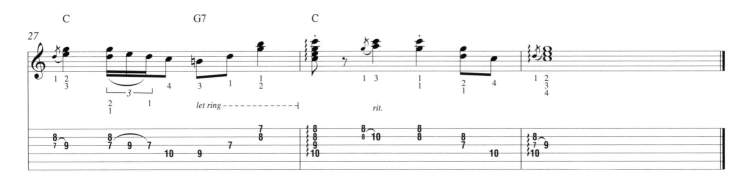

Funky Monkey

This solo focuses on the funky side of double stops. Lots of ♭7ths, ♭3rds, and ♭5ths help to get that funky, swampy sound. Use hybrid picking to make these licks pop. Check out the great Jerry Reed on nylon string guitar—arguably the originator of this style in tunes like "The Claw" and "Blue Finger."

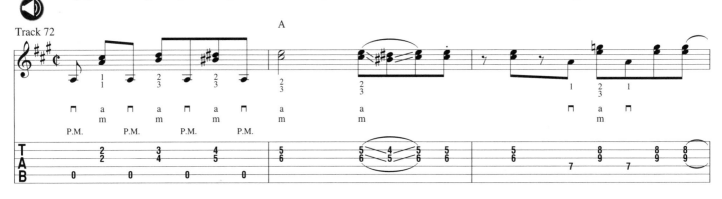

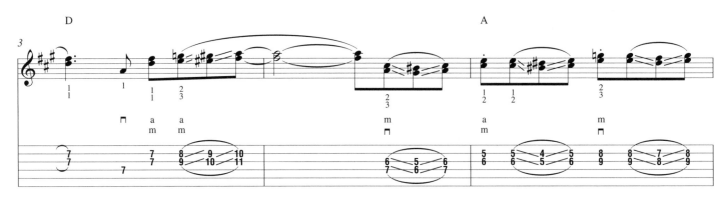

Chapter Nine: Double Stops

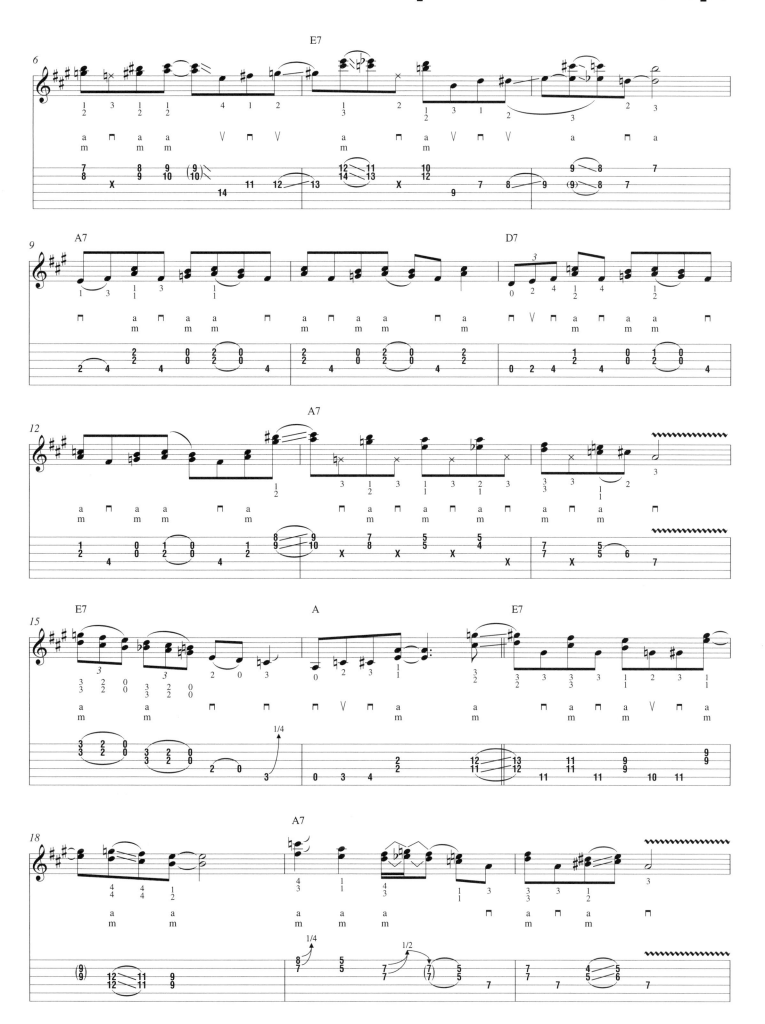

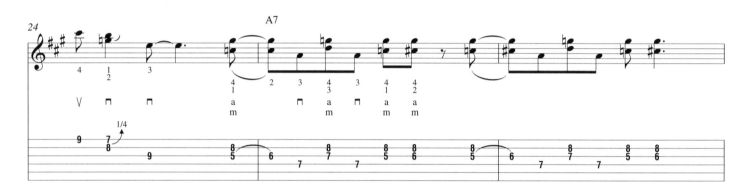

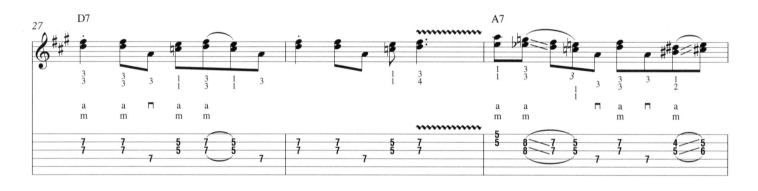

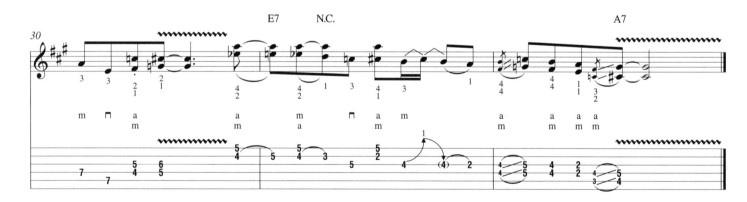

Chapter Ten: 10 Triad Basics

The best way to improve your soloing in any style of guitar playing is to learn your chords! Having a good sense of how chords work in different keys is the most important bit of music theory you need to learn as a complete musician, as well as a country guitar player. To understand this concept, you must first learn to harmonize major scales with triads. In this chapter, we'll touch on the basics as they relate to country guitar, but I would encourage you to get a few more music theory books and really nail this concept down.

Let's start by learning the notes of a basic C major scale.

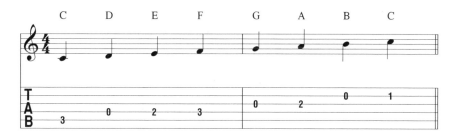

Now harnonize the scale in 3rds to get the following triads. A triad is a three-note chord. Assign a Roman numeral to each chord.

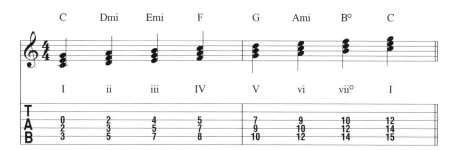

This triad pattern repeats in every key to give you the diatonic chords in any key. For example, in the key of F, the diatonic chords are as follows:

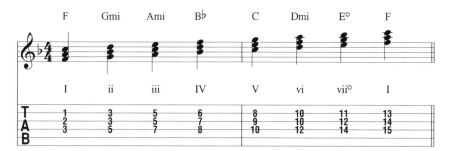

In other words, the I chord is always major, the ii always minor, the V always major, etc.—no matter what key you are in. This is the diatonic chord pattern for any key. You should transpose the pattern and learn to move the chords to different keys, different areas of the neck, and different string sets.

You can rearrange the veritcal order of the notes to create different inversions.

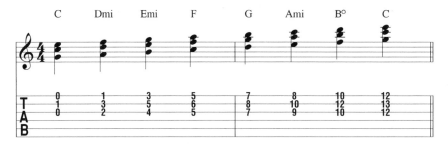

Use your open chords to get a starting point and harmonize the scale with that voicing.
Here's the key of E on strings 3–1, followed by the same harmonized scale on strings 4–2.

This is G major on strings 4–2, followed by the same harmonized scale on strings 5–3.

Continue this concept with all triad inversions in different keys and on different string sets. You are learning all the chords to every key up and down the fingerboard.

Triads and Country Guitar

The reason for learning this concept is that the most solid notes to use in your solos are the ones that belong to whatever chord or triad you happen to be playing over. For example, if you are playing a song in the key of C and are on a C chord, the safest notes are that of a C triad: C, E, and G. If the chord changes to F, the triad notes are now F, A, and C.

These are the *chord tones.* You are playing the harmony of the song—not just your stock memorized licks. If you learn to play chord tones up and down the neck in every key, your playing will improve 110 percent. Of course, there are many other notes that you can play to make your solos more exciting and interesting, but you should learn the rules before you break them!

By strengthening the harmonic content of your soloing and learning to follow the chords, every solo becomes unique and more interesting because the chord progression and harmony of every individual song are different. Learn to morph your ideas and change a few notes to use them over different chords and chord shapes.

Also, many times in country music—especially in traditional country—playing the melody of the song with a few embellishments makes for a great solo. You'll find that most of these melodies are based off the chord tones. I'd suggest taking some classic country tunes from artists like Hank Williams or Merle Haggard, learning the chords, and then learning the melodies so you can pick out the chord tones.

A strong, working knowledge of triads and all chord shapes is perhaps the single most important ingredient to good country guitar playing. Whether playing a melodic solo, blistering 16th notes, a steel guitar bending lick, a rhythm part, or some tasty backup fills, an awareness of the nearest triad position will give your playing a solid home base to which you can always resolve.

Buckersfield

This Don Rich-inspired tune demonstrates one way to use triads and chord shapes (Don was the guitarist for Buck Owens). The idea is to grab a chord and play out of that shape, adding a few notes and rhythmic variations to create an interesting solo or rhythm part. When the chord changes, you grab a new hand position.

The chord diagrams give you the basic triad shape from which you're working. It's played with a pick, although you could work in hybrid picking, as well. At bars 17–22, open strings are used for a jangly guitar sound.

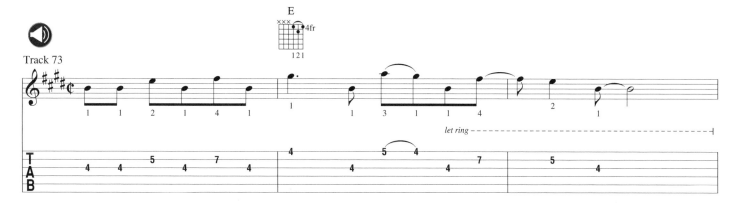

Track 73

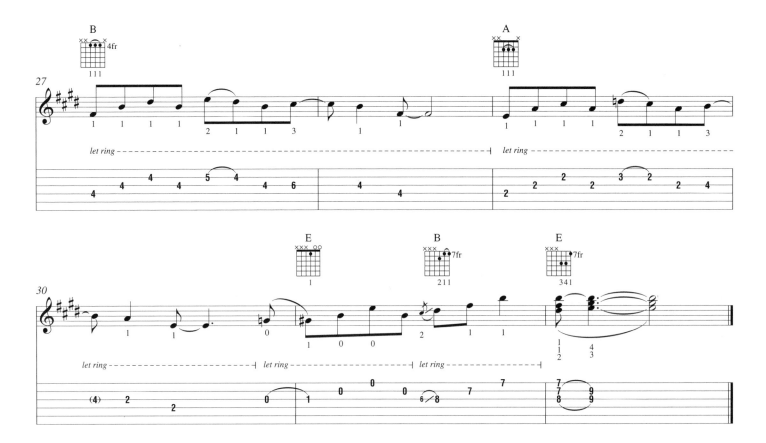

Triad Pull-offs

This technique utilizes a series of pull-offs within a triad form. The resultant sound creates a little tension, which is then resolved to a more stable sound. This concept is very useful for playing over a fast two-beat feel. The following examples demonstrate a few different sounds. Hybrid picking works well and sounds punchy, but a pick-only approach sounds good, too.

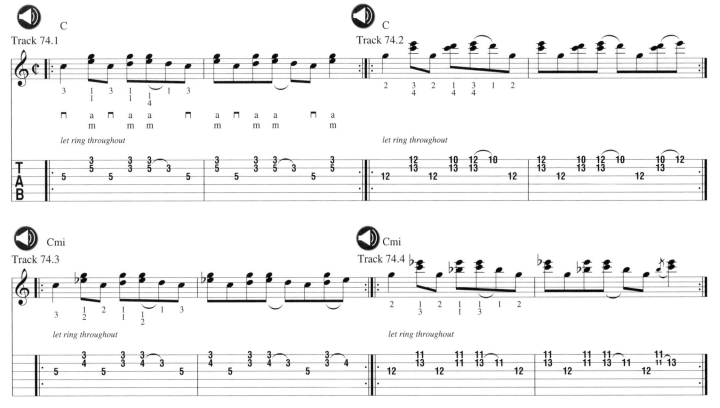

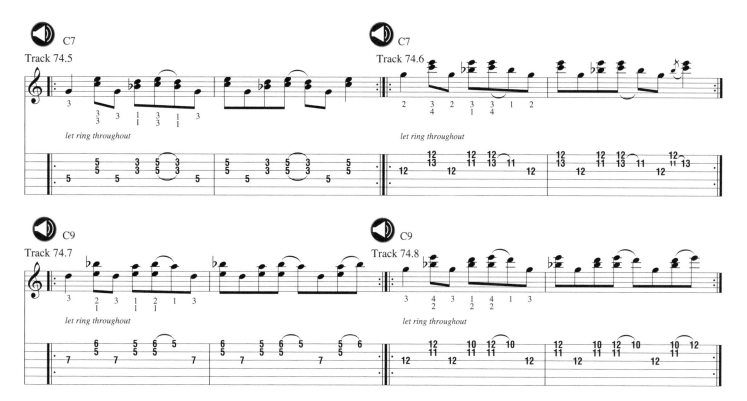

The use of triads and chord tones is a huge subject and cannot be fully covered in this book. Take the material presented here and use it as a springboard for you to further explore the subject on your own through other books and listening, which ultimately will be your best teacher. Check out the solo by Brent Mason on "Pop a Top" by Alan Jackson for an excellent example of chord-tone usage.

Pickin' Time

This tune makes use of chord tones and triad pull-offs.

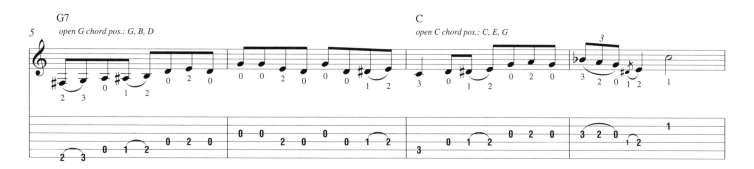

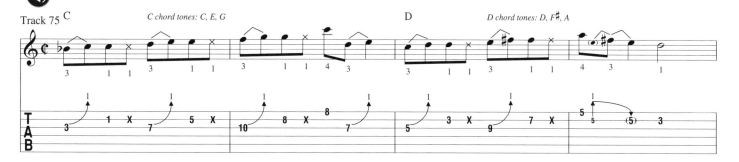

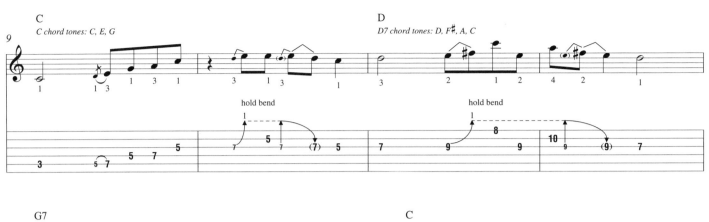

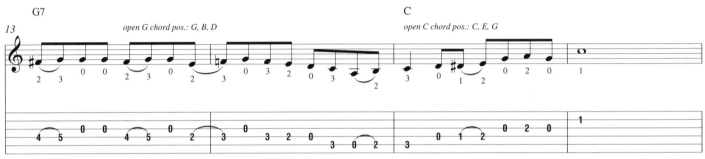

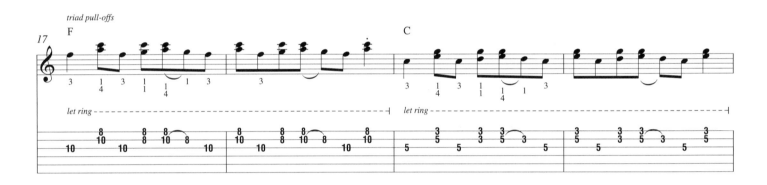

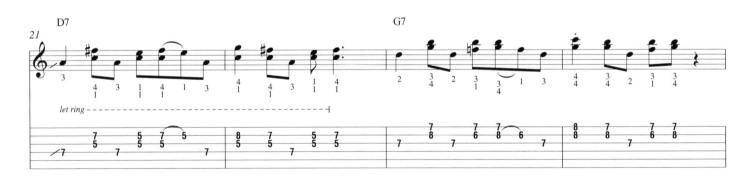

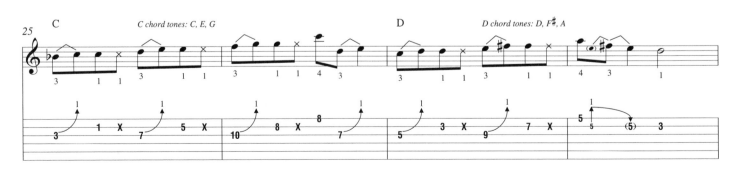

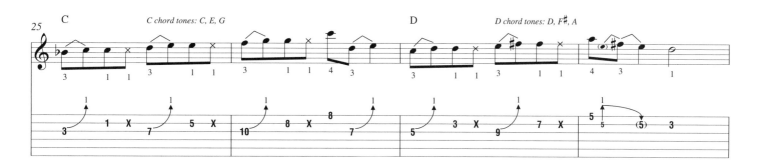

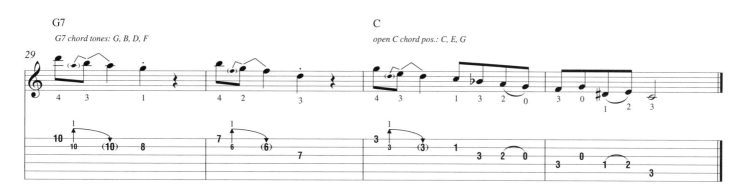

Chapter Eleven: Banjo Rolls

11

In addition to pedal-steel emulation, country guitar pickers often like to incorporate banjo-style ideas into their playing. A banjo is normally played with a thumbpick and two or three fingers on your right hand. To get this rolling effect on guitar, we use the pick-and-roll technique via hybrid picking and open-string scales (see Chapter 4 for a more detailed explanation of hybrid picking).

For banjo rolls on the guitar, the idea is to find a pick-and-roll pattern that works through the chords of the song, using open strings whenever possible. Also try to keep a pedal note ringing to emulate a five-string banjo; the root note or 5th of the key usually work best. Let common tones ring through all the chords, and don't be afraid of a little dissonance at times, as it can create some nice effects.

Here's a simple but very usable example of a banjo roll in the key of G. Play the rolls slowly and accurately at first, building speed over time. Regarding the right-hand notation, ⊓ = downstroke with the pick, *m* = middle finger, and *a* = ring finger.

Track 76.1 G

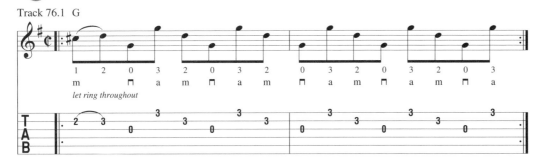

Here's a similar banjo roll in the key of E.

Track 76.2 E

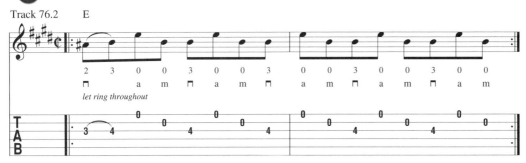

Here's a banjo roll in the key of C using no open strings. It can get awkward on the left hand when trying to keep a pedal note ringing. Make sure you hold the notes down and let them ring into each other.

Track 76.3 C

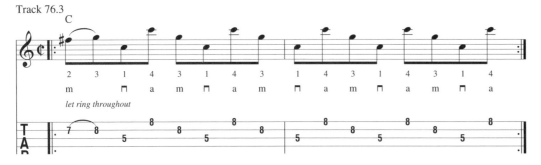

Rocky Roll

This tune demonstrates various ways to keep the banjo rolls going through the changes of a standard country chord progression. Note the use of some standard banjo-type phrases that depart from the rolling technique.

At bar 18, there's a difficult bend. Try to use your first finger for support behind your second finger as you bend the A note on the third string. Bend it up a half step and hold it as you roll through the other notes, letting them ring into each other. The combination of the E, D, and B♭ notes and a C in the bass gives you a C9 sound.

At bar 20, there's a similar lick and bend, but this time, you bend up a whole step from A to B, resulting in a G major sound. Pay close attention to all picking patterns and left-hand fingerings. Try working on one or two bars at a time to start. As always, start slowly and try to keep your hands relaxed as you eventually build up speed.

Track 77

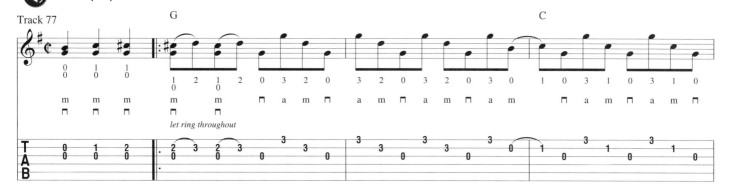

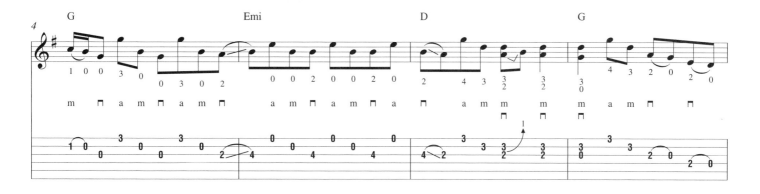

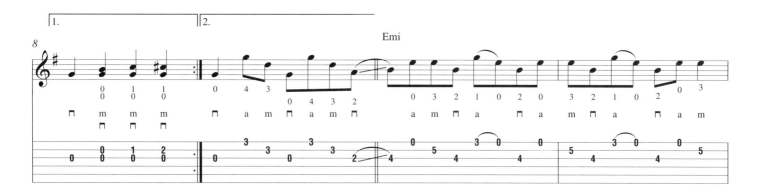

Chapter Twelve: 12 Open-String Cascades

Incorporating open strings into a scale can produce a unique "cascading" or harp-like sound that's a very effective device in country guitar playing. The technique involves playing a scale or lick with open strings wherever possible and letting the notes ring toegether for as long as possible.

You can play these ideas with standard flatpicking, but this technique works best using hybrid picking. Your left-hand fingerings will have to make adjustments and some uncommon stretches at times. Keep your left-hand fingers arched and on the fingertips so they stay clear of adjacent strings.

Check out Jerry Reed and Chet Atkins on "Jerry's Breakdown," as well as Albert Lee on "T-Bird to Vegas" to hear good use of this effect.

Best Keys for Open-string Scales

The keys of G, C, A, D, and E work best with this technique because of the notes available on the open strings of the guitar. If you're playing a song in a different key and want to use open strings, you can use a capo. Sometimes you have to force an open string to work over a chord by combining it with other notes and resolving it in order to get the desired effect. You should approach each chord and key differently, as each one has its own characteristics when played with open strings.

The following examples are played at a slower tempo so you can hear and work out the notes. To get the full effect, you should speed these up, as in the tune "Cascade Town."

This G major pentatonic scale is a good starting point.

Track 78.1

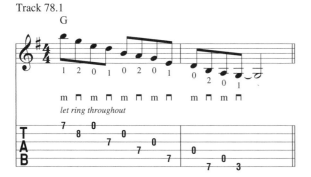

We can add a pull-off to the same scale as an alternate method.

Track 78.2

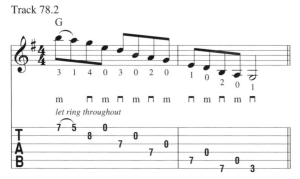

Because of the nature of the way these scales sound, you can take great liberty with the harmonic content. Adding notes outside of the diatonic harmony can be used to create dissonance, which sounds good when resolved properly. You're also not restricted to scales that move straight up or down; you can mix up the order of the notes to accomodate fingerings, picking patterns, melodic flow, or whatever else you need to make it work. Learn these examples slowly, paying close attention to the fingerings, and then speed up for the best effect.

This example demonstrates a funky, dissonant G7 run.

Track 78.3

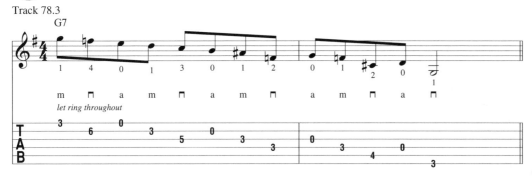

Here's a classic, dissonant Merle Travis lick in G.

Track 78.4

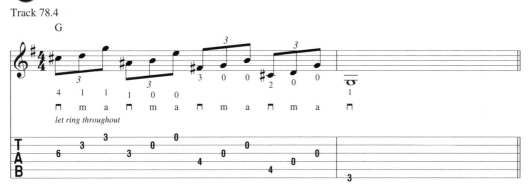

Let's look at a few more examples in diffrent keys. This one is in the key of A.

Track 78.5

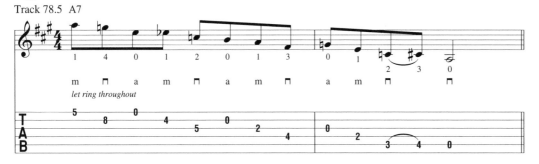

Here's one that suggests C7.

Track 78.6

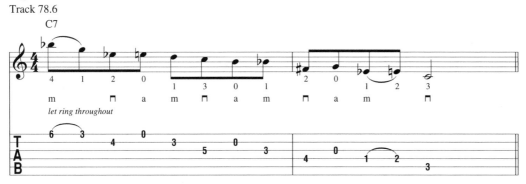

And here are two in the key of D.

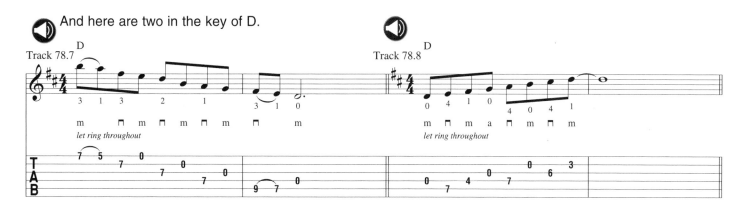

Cascade Town

This tune makes use of many open-string cascading ideas. Make sure that you examine how each lick works over the corresponding chord. It's played on the recording at a fast tempo. Learn each idea very slowly, paying attention to both left- and right-hand fingerings, and gradually build up the speed. You may also approach each bar as an independent lick, eventually learning to go smoothly from one idea to the next.

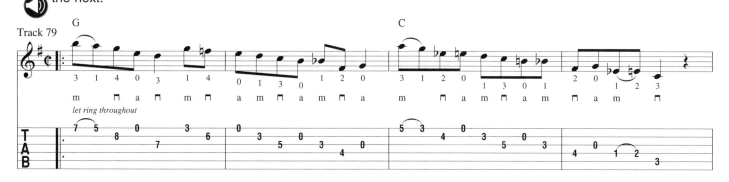

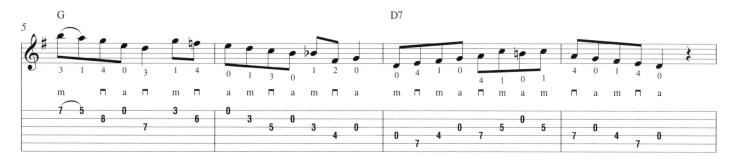

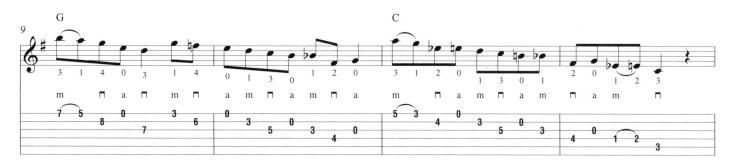

Chapter Thirteen:
13 Cow Jazz

"Texas swing," "Western swing," "country swing," and "cow jazz" are all terms for the jazzier side of country music. This style combines elements of traditional jazz and big band swing with down-home country roots music and instrumentation. The result is its own breed of country music, which musicians love to play. It's quite a lot of fun jamming on classic tunes like "San Antonio Rose" or "Milk Cow Blues."

A classic Western swing band would have a rhythm section, along with two fiddlers, a steel guitar, piano, electric guitar, and, at times, a horn section. The arrangements feature many harmonized lines and rhythmic accents, much like a jazz big band.

The guitar players are expected to have solid rhythm chops and a very good chord vocabulary, along with the ability to solo over the chord changes while blending elements of country, traditional jazz, and blues. Artists like Bob Wills and the Texas Playboys, Hank Thompson, Spade Cooley, Asleep at the Wheel, and the Time Jumpers offer up a wide range of recordings. Other country artists, like George Straight, Merle Haggard, and Lyle Lovett, have been known to include some swing tunes in their repertoire.

Traditional guitarists Eldon Shamblin, Jimmy Wyble, Hank Garland, Billy Byrd, and Jimmy Bryant can be heard on classic country swing recordings. Modern players like Scotty Anderson, Brent Mason, and Red Volkaert also have some nice swinging tunes on their solo albums.

Jazz guitarists Charlie Christian, Django Reinhardt, and Wes Montgomery all played amazing stuff that translates very well to Western swing and have influenced most of the guitarists in this style. Like any other style, it's very important to listen to the music to fully grasp its feel and subtleties.

Swing Shift

This tune demonstrates how to play over chord changes by concentrating on the chord tones and using all the elements mentioned. Also, some altered scale ideas are used over some of the 7th chords, which creates a little tension and resolution. The tune also makes use of some *chords clusters*, which are a common sound in this style.

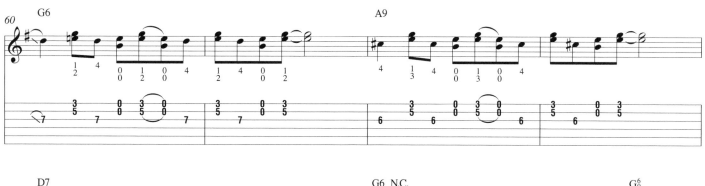

Swingin' in San Antone (Rhythm with a Moving Bass Line)

In Western swing, rhythm guitar parts are often played with a melodic bass line moving beneath the chord progression. Sometimes you can work out parts with the bass player, but it can sound good when the parts are different and harmonizing with each other, as well. Eldon Shamblin (from Bob Wills and the Texas Playboys) is considered the master of this style of rhythm playing. Also, Freddie Green (from the Count Basie Orchestra) used this style in a jazz big band context.

Chords may be substituted within the basic progression to accomodate the bass part as long as they resolve to the next chord. Two- and three-note open-voiced chords on the lower strings work well for this style. The following example uses a standard Texas swing chord progression to demonstrate a moving bass part. The top row of chord symbols reflects the standard chord progression, while the bottom row indicates the substitutions used.

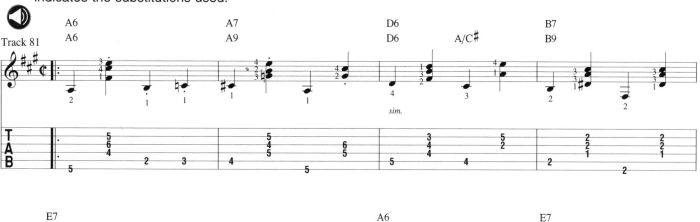

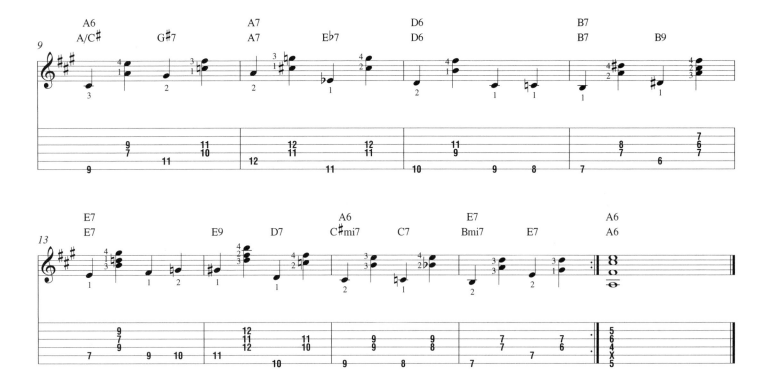

Chapter Fourteen: Intros and Endings

14

One of the main functions of the lead guitar player in a country band is to play good, solid intros and endings. A well-played intro sets the groove, tempo, and general approach that the band will lock into. You may find yourself performing or recording with a group in which you will be asked to come up with a suitable part on the spot. In such cases, it's a good idea to have stockpiled a number of intros and endings that will work in many different situations. You can take those ideas and customize them to fit the song you are playing by changing a few notes, changing the feel, etc.

In traditional country, it's a good idea to sometimes quote part of the melody of the song, the last two or three bars of the chorus, or another recognizable hook from the tune when playing the intro. Once you learn a few standard ideas, it becomes easier to come up with your own creative variations, combining all the different styles and techniques with which you're familiar.

Many modern country songs tend to rely on a unique riff or melody that sets the tone of the song and may be repeated throughout. Note that many intros will start with a pickup measure before the actual chord progression of the intro. Also, the last bar of many intros will include a walk-up riff or some other kind of lead-in to the first verse or chorus.

Country musicians will call out the key and the intro chords using the Nashville Number System to communicate with other members of the band. This is similar to the Roman numeral system, but it uses standard numbers instead. For instance, in the key of C, a 1 5 1 1 would be C G C C.

Intros

Here are some examples of intros using the most common intro chord progressions that you would hear on the bandstand at your friendly neighborhood Honky Tonk bar.

Intro #1: 1 5 1 1

This example is a steel-guitar-sounding intro to a slow-tempo ballad.

Track 82

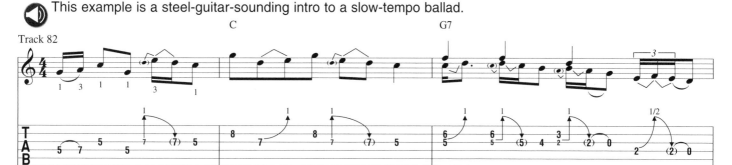

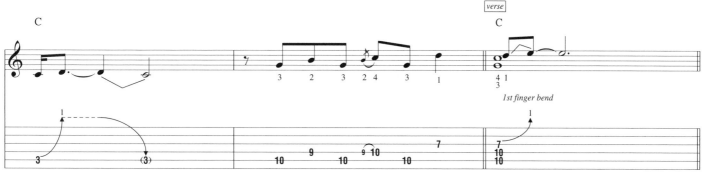

Intro #2: 1 5 1 5

This example works well over a mid-tempo shuffle rhythm. Note the anticipated first beat of the walk-up measure. This "push" is very common in country music.

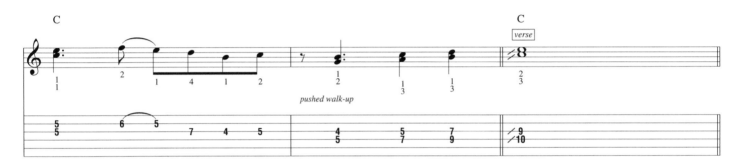

Intro #3: 1 5 1 1

This rockin' intro over a train beat sets up a nice feel for the song. Try hybrid picking.

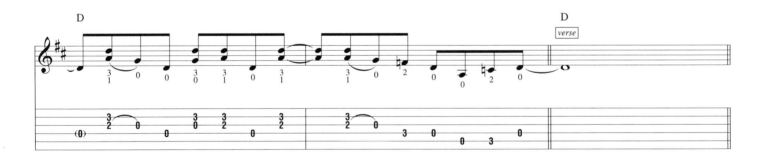

Intro #4: 5 5 1 1

This intro works well on a number of traditional country standards.

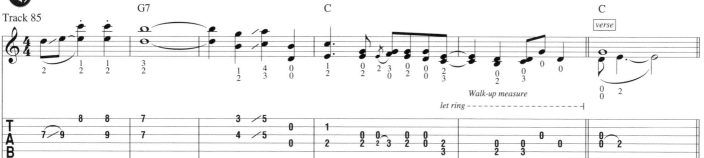

Intro #5: 2 5 1 1

This Bakersfield-style chicken-pickin' intro starts right on the II chord; there's no pickup bar.

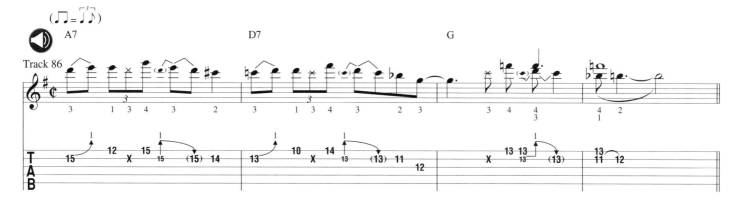

Intro #6: 4 5 1 1

Playing 3rds with an added lower octave gives the impression of a chord-melody sound.

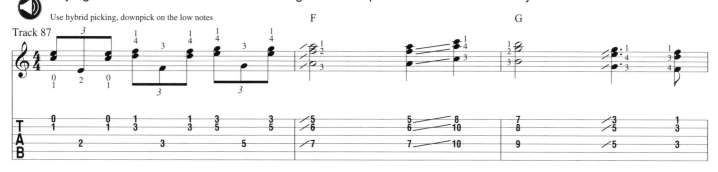

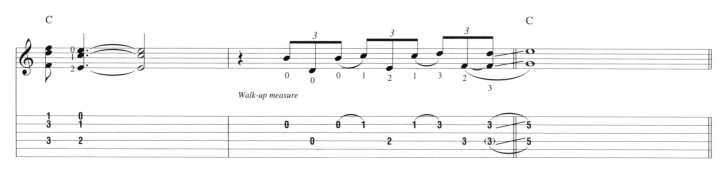

Intro #7: Rock 'n' Roll

Many contemporary country tunes have a rock 'n' roll attitude and a driving beat. This Chuck Berry-inspired intro kicks the song into high gear from the first riff. Try using all downstrokes for the best effect.

Intro #8: I-chord Vamp

This intro is over a static I chord in E. It starts with a banjo roll, goes into a sequenced E7 scale pattern, and ends with a funky, hybrid-picked rhythm pattern, all at a fast two-beat tempo. Vamp on the last two bars until the vocal or melody of the tune starts. Note the use of pull-offs at bar 5. This is a good way to fake it when you find yourself in a little over your head when playing at a blisteringly fast tempo! (In other words, trying to keep up with the hot fiddle player!) Experiment with hybrid picking in bars 5–8.

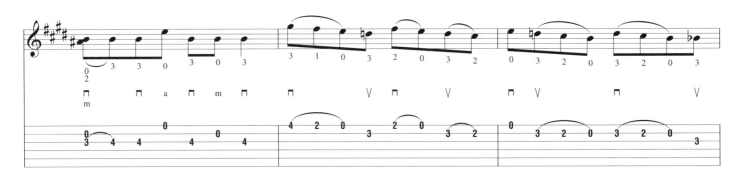

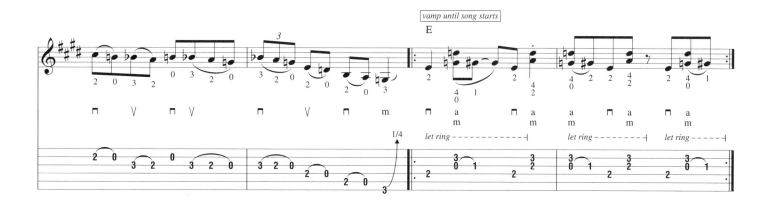

Obviously, there can be a custom intro lick or riff for every song. So be creative and ready whenever you are called upon to kick the tune off!

Endings

A good country ending lick should sum up the essence of the tune you are playing and add an unmistakable finality to the song. A V–I (or 5 1) cadence in the last bar is very common and works well. You can get very creative on endings in a rehearsed situation by adding syncopated rhythms or chords that take the tune to a new place.

As with intros, you should always have a stock ending ready to go if you're called upon with short notice. Many times, an ending will start with the tag of the song, followed by a strong final lick. Here are some examples of endings that would work over many country songs.

Ending #1

This bluegrass lick ends more tunes than any other.

Track 90.1

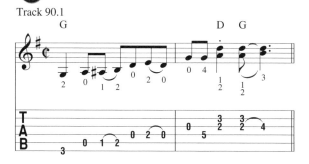

Here's the same lick with a bend.

Track 90.2

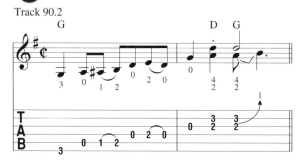

Ending #2

Here's a standard Bakersfield-style ending. Use hybrid picking for a punchy, chiken-pickin' sound. Try using different voicings of the same triads for a variation.

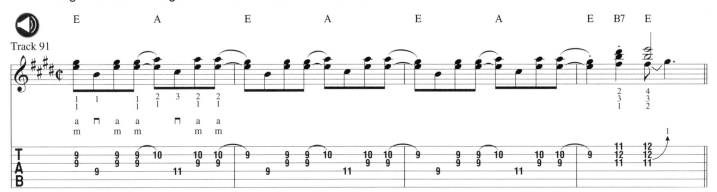

Ending #3

This rockabilly ending starts with a double-stop, quarter-step bend and works down a blues scale.

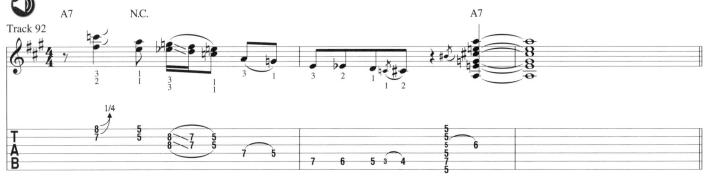

Ending #4

Here's an ending for a Texas swing tune in the style of Bob Wills, with a couple of different possibilities for the last two bars. Note the jazzy chord to end the second lick.

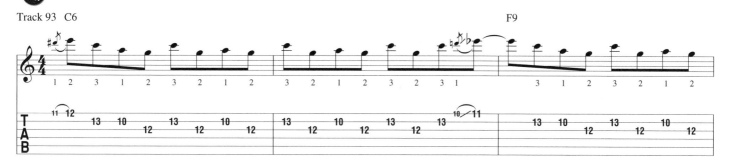

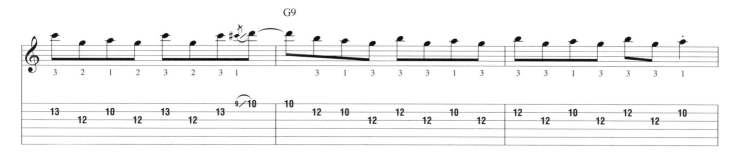

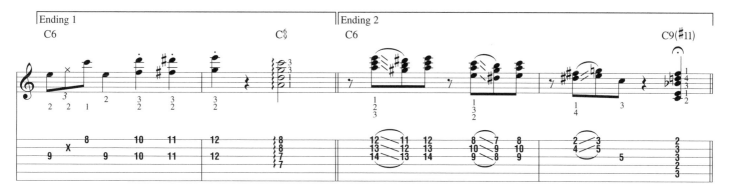

Ending #5

On this legato steel guitar ending, let the notes ring together and gradually ritard. Intonation on the pre-bends is very important. Pick the notes softly to avoid tuning problems.

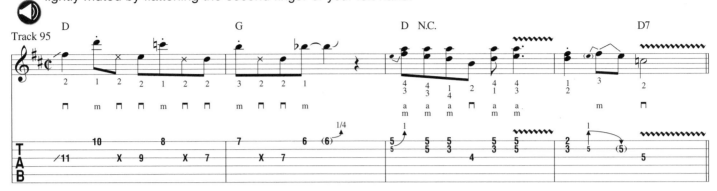

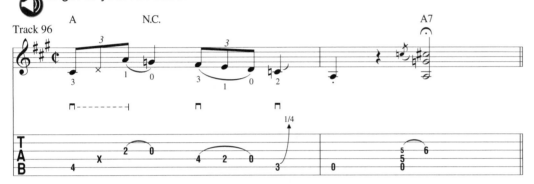

Ending #6

This chicken-pickin' ending lick requires hybrid picking for full effect. In bars 1–2, the second string is lightly muted by flattening the second finger of your left hand.

Ending #7

The band stops, and you play this. Try it with hybrid picking, too. The fourth string is muted with the third finger of your left hand.

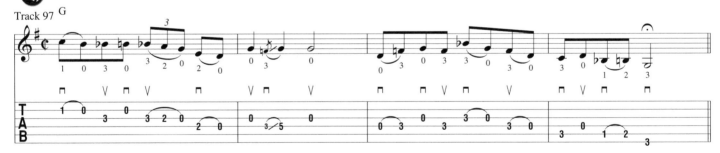

Ending #8

Here's a flatpicking ending in open G position.

Chapter Fifteen: Scale Patterns

Presented here are the most common and usable scale patterns as they relate to country guitar playing. All of these patterns are movable. The root in the patterns are circled.

Major Scale Caged System Patterns

Here are the 5 basic CAGED System major scale patterns which can also be transposed to minor keys or different modes.

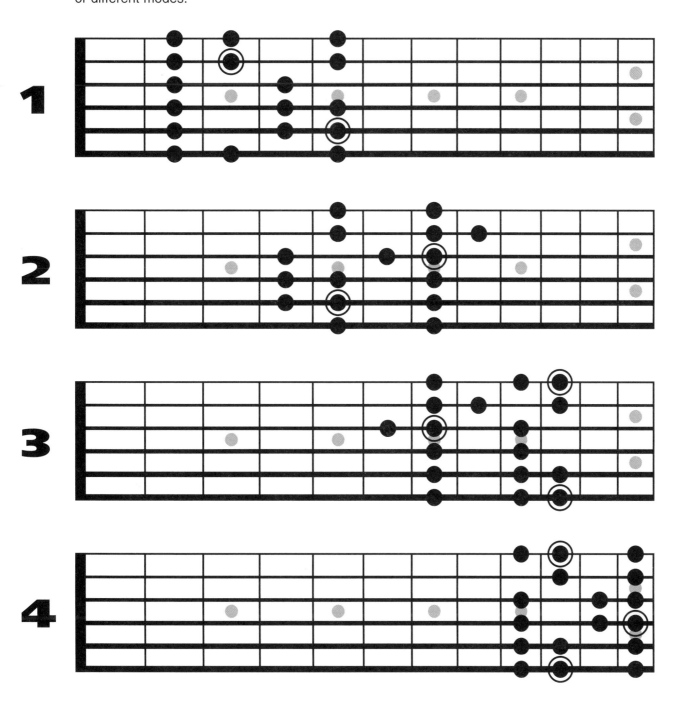

5

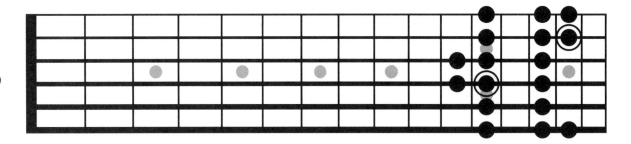

Major Pentatonic Patterns

6-String root extended major pentatonic

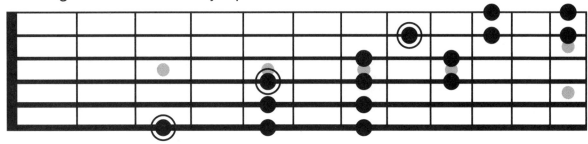

5-String root CAGED pattern

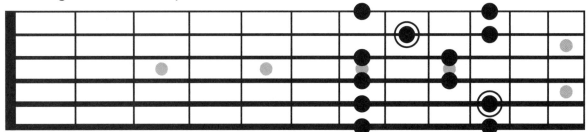

5-String root extended major pentatonic

6-String root CAGED pattern

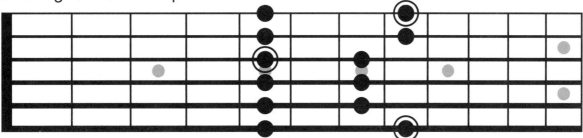

Minor Pentatonic Patterns

6-String root extended minor pentatonic

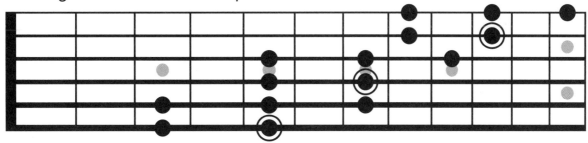

6-String root CAGED pattern

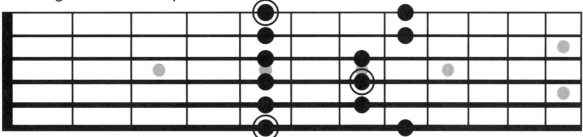

5-String root extended minor pentatonic

5-String root CAGED pattern

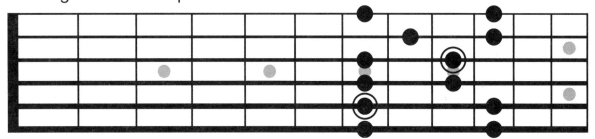

Natural Minor Patterns

6-String root natural minor

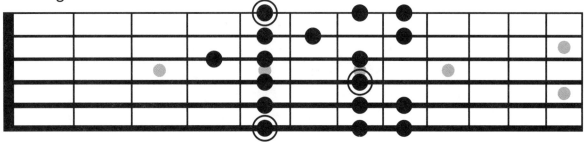

5-String root natural minor

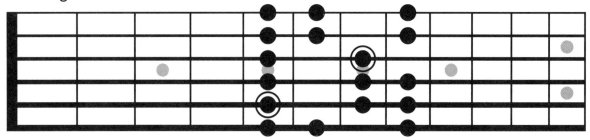

Dorian Minor

6-String root Dorian minor

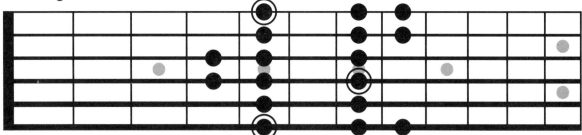

5-String root Dorian minor

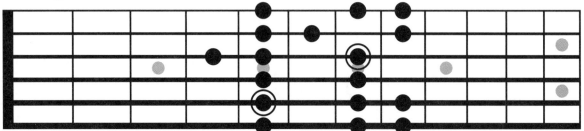

Harmonic Minor

6-String root harmonic minor

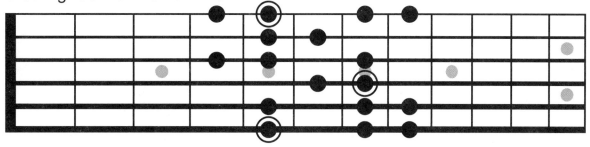

5-String root harmonic minor

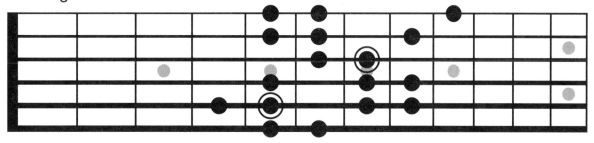

Mixolydian

6-String root Mixolydian

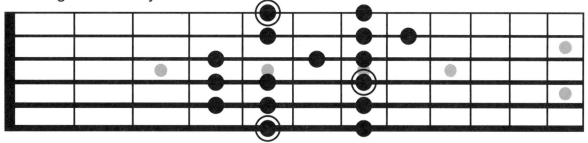

5-String root Mixolydian

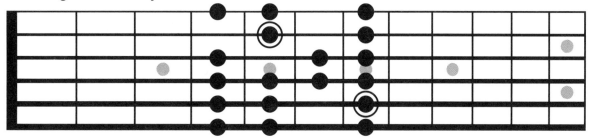

MUSICIANS INSTITUTE PRESS is the official series of Southern California's renowned music school, Musicians Institute. MI instructors, some of the finest musicians in the world, share their vast knowledge and experience with you – no matter what your current level. For guitar, bass, drums, vocals, and keyboards, MI Press offers the finest music curriculum for higher learning through a variety of series:

ESSENTIAL CONCEPTS
Designed from MI core curriculum programs.

MASTER CLASS
Designed from MI elective courses.

PRIVATE LESSONS
Tackle a variety of topics "one-on one" with MI faculty instructors.

GUITAR

Acoustic Artistry
by Evan Hirschelman • Private Lessons
00695922 Book/Online Audio $19.99

Advanced Scale Concepts & Licks for Guitar
by Jean Marc Belkadi • Private Lessons
00695298 Book/CD Pack $16.95

Basic Blues Guitar
by Steve Trovato • Private Lessons
00695180 Book/CD Pack $15.99

Blues/Rock Soloing for Guitar
by Robert Calva • Private Lessons
00695680 Book/CD Pack $19.99

Blues Guitar Soloing
by Keith Wyatt • Master Class
00695132 Book/Online Audio $24.99

Blues Rhythm Guitar
by Keith Wyatt • Master Class
00695131 Book/Online Audio $19.95

Dean Brown
00696002 DVD $29.95

Chord Progressions for Guitar
by Tom Kolb • Private Lessons
00695664 Book/CD Pack $17.99

Chord Tone Soloing
by Barrett Tagliarino • Private Lessons
00695855 Book/CD Pack $24.99

Chord-Melody Guitar
by Bruce Buckingham • Private Lessons
00695646 Book/CD Pack $17.99

Classical & Fingerstyle Guitar Techniques
by David Oakes • Master Class
00695171 Book/CD Pack $17.99

Classical Themes for Electric Guitar
by Jean Marc Belkadi • Private Lessons
00695806 Book/CD Pack $15.99

Contemporary Acoustic Guitar
by Eric Paschal & Steve Trovato • Master Class
00695320 Book/CD Pack $16.95

Creative Chord Shapes
by Jamie Findlay • Private Lessons
00695172 Book/CD Pack $10.99

Diminished Scale for Guitar
by Jean Marc Belkadi • Private Lessons
00695227 Book/CD Pack $10.99

Essential Rhythm Guitar
by Steve Trovato • Private Lessons
00695181 Book/CD Pack $15.99

Ethnic Rhythms for Electric Guitar
by Jean Marc Belkadi • Private Lessons
00695873 Book/CD Pack $17.99

Exotic Scales & Licks for Electric Guitar
by Jean Marc Belkadi • Private Lessons
00695860 Book/CD Pack $16.95

Funk Guitar
by Ross Bolton • Private Lessons
00695419 Book/CD Pack $15.99

Guitar Basics
by Bruce Buckingham • Private Lessons
00695134 Book/CD Pack $17.99

Guitar Fretboard Workbook
by Barrett Tagliarino • Essential Concepts
00695712 . . . . $19.99

Guitar Hanon
by Peter Deneff • Private Lessons
00695321 . . . . $9.95

Guitar Lick•tionary
by Dave Hill • Private Lessons
00695482 Book/CD Pack $19.99

Guitar Soloing
by Dan Gilbert & Beth Marlis • Essential Concepts
00695190 Book/CD Pack $22.99
00695907 DVD $19.95

Harmonics
by Jamie Findlay • Private Lessons
00695169 Book/CD Pack $13.99

Introduction to Jazz Guitar Soloing
by Joe Elliott • Master Class
00695406 Book/CD Pack $19.95

Jazz Guitar Chord System
by Scott Henderson • Private Lessons
00695291 . . . . $12.99

Jazz Guitar Improvisation
by Sid Jacobs • Master Class
00695128 Book/CD Pack $18.99
00695908 DVD $19.95
00695639 VHS Video $19.95

Jazz-Rock Triad Improvising
by Jean Marc Belkadi • Private Lessons
00695361 Book/CD Pack $15.99

Latin Guitar
by Bruce Buckingham • Master Class
00695379 Book/CD Pack $17.99

Liquid Legato
by Allen Hinds • Private Lessons
00696656 Book/CD Pack $14.99

Modern Approach to Jazz, Rock & Fusion Guitar
by Jean Marc Belkadi • Private Lessons
00695143 Book/CD Pack $15.99

Modern Jazz Concepts for Guitar
by Sid Jacobs • Master Class
00695711 Book/CD Pack $16.95

Modern Rock Rhythm Guitar
by Danny Gill • Private Lessons
00695682 Book/CD Pack $16.95

Modes for Guitar
by Tom Kolb • Private Lessons
00695555 Book/Online Audio $18.99

Music Reading for Guitar
by David Oakes • Essential Concepts
00695192 . . . . $19.99

Outside Guitar Licks
by Jean Marc Belkadi • Private Lessons
00695697 Book/CD Pack $16.99

Power Plucking
by Dale Turner • Private Lesson
00695962 . . . . $19.95

Progressive Tapping Licks
by Jean Marc Belkadi • Private Lessons
00695748 Book/CD Pack $15.95

Rhythm Guitar
by Bruce Buckingham & Eric Paschal • Essential Concepts
00695188 Book $17.95
00114559 Book/Online Audio $24.99
00695909 DVD $19.95

Rhythmic Lead Guitar
by Barrett Tagliarino • Private Lessons
00110263 Book/CD Pack $19.99

Rock Lead Basics
by Nick Nolan & Danny Gill • Master Class
00695144 Book/CD Pack $18.99
00695910 DVD $19.95

Rock Lead Performance
by Nick Nolan & Danny Gill • Master Class
00695278 Book/CD Pack $17.95

Rock Lead Techniques
by Nick Nolan & Danny Gill • Master Class
00695146 Book/CD Pack $16.99

Shred Guitar
by Greg Harrison • Master Class
00695977 Book/CD Pack $19.99

Slap & Pop Technique for Guitar
00695645 Book/CD Pack $14.99

Technique Exercises for Guitar
by Jean Marc Belkadi • Private Lessons
00695913 . . . . $15.99

Texas Blues Guitar
by Robert Calva • Private Lessons
00695340 Book/CD Pack $17.95

Ultimate Guitar Technique
by Bill LaFleur • Private Lessons
00695863 . . . . $22.99

Prices, contents, and availability subject to change without notice.

HAL•LEONARD®
C O R P O R A T I O N
7777 W. BLUEMOUND RD. P.O. BOX 13819 MILWAUKEE, WI 53213
www.halleonard.com

0516